Children of Healing

Learning to trust God through loss, pregnancy and adoption.

Karrie Ann Manning

Dedication

To ALL my children,

Those who are walking on the Earth, and those who are waiting for us all to arrive at the party.

Thanks

I would like to take a moment to say a huge Thank You to my husband, John, for all his support. He has not only walked through the jungles of book writing and publishing with me, but he has also been with me through ALL life's ups and downs. We have learned much together. I would not wish to do this life with anyone other than you. I Love You Babe.

Contents

Children of Healing

The Diagnosis

Nineteen years old, a year of marriage, eleven pregnancy tests later and finding myself now sitting in a doctor's office trying to wrap my head around what she had just said. *Was she serious? Did she laugh as she said it? What will I tell my husband? Oh God, I am a failure... again....?*

I am sure I was polite as I wrapped up the appointment, but the rest of the conversation is a blur to me. I think I was given information about PCOS but I don't recall. The truth was I had never heard of it before.

It you have not heard of this it is short for Poly Cystic Ovary Syndrome. It is mainly characterized by multiple cysts on in the ovaries which lead to hormone imbalances. Hormone imbalances can lead to so many difficulties, as we women seem to have all our bodily functions tied to hormones; including, but not limited to, getting pregnant. The diagnosis was confirmed with the ultrasound by looking at my ovaries.

It certainly explained my whole life to this point, but it was not the news I was prepared for. And above all that I was certainly not prepared for the attitude of the doctor delivering the news. I managed to get myself to the safety of my car before the tears began to flow uncontrollably.

I had a forty-five-minute drive home and I am not sure how I made it. I cried. I screamed. I argued. I bargained. And, I replayed the doctor's words over and over and over in my head. She had said we would, "probably never have children on our own. Oh, you can try and let nature take its course, *but*, when you are truly serious about having kids you come see us, we will give you what you need to make it happen."

As I look back on it, maybe she thought her words were helpful; however, at the time they felt like stabbing wounds to the gut. And the smile on her face felt like a mocking gesture, there was certainly no warmth in it at all. As I made the drive home I knew there would be questions, questions that now I did not want to face. I did not even drive home. I drove straight to my husband, John, or rather, to his work place and sat waiting for his shift to get over. He was just as surprised to see me there as I was that my car actually led me there.

I desperately needed the strong embrace of his arms; yet as I cried into his chest for a moment I tried also to push away as I shared with him the news the doctor had just weighed me down with. I told him he should divorce me now because I could never give him children. Being much more level headed, and not the one with crazy hormone levels, he informed me that I was being ridiculous, which of course I was. But in my mind, this was devastating news. He hugged me tighter and said, "Right now you are going to focus on school, get through graduation and the state exam and you of all people know what God can do."

Yes, I did. I had heard the story my whole life, of how the Lord had healed my momma after five years of her struggle with infertility. How after her doctors had given up on her, the Lord called her to a full gospel church and how she had been prayed for and how God showed up. She gave birth to my twin brother and me. Yes, I knew the story. I knew what God could do. Why, in those moments did it seem that He could not, or was it my fear that He would not, which caused the tears to flow so hard?

We went home to share the news with our families as they all knew about the appointment. My mom of course rejected all notions of what the doctor had said. Because you see, she knew what her God could do. She prayed right then for a child to prove this doctor wrong. The very next Sunday with my parents and his parents surrounding us, we were prayed over again by the Pastor of our church. I knew God could do this, but I will admit I was still not sure He would.

Over the next few days we discussed what should be done. The doctor wanted to put me back on a birth control pill just to level out the hormones and keep my body functioning like it should. I understood and yet I had struggled so badly during the last year trying to find one that did not have horrible side effects for me that we had given up on them. We had decided that if a baby came now it would be ok. But, now being faced with having to use them, made the idea even more repulsive to me. I knew I needed to do something, but I did not like either of my options. I threw most of my energy into finishing nursing school. Also, at this time, my parents were moving back across the country and taking most all our things with them. Up to this point we had all been sharing a very big three story, old Victorian home. Our plan was also to move west when I finished school. So, in the meantime, we moved in with John's parents and youngest brother in their apartment for the next three months. There was so much going on that I had decided to just ignore and put up with my body for the time being.

Now, it is important before continuing on with this story that you understand something. I was raised in a loving Christian home with both a Christian mother and father. Was life always perfect? Of course not. But, I knew they loved me. I knew I was a miracle child. I knew God was real and that His word was true. I knew He lived in my heart and that I did my very best to please Him. I would even go so far as to tell you I could argue all the right Christian answers to all life's hard questions. I could quote scripture for you and was very involved in church activities and outreaches. I would even tell you that *I Loved the Lord* with all my heart. About now you are wondering where the "but" comes in. You are right, there was a critical piece missing in my heart. I believed God loved everyone and that He had a plan for them, but somehow in my heart of hearts I didn't think He meant me. He must have really meant all those other more perfect people or the really, really, pitiful ones that needed His mercy. Deep in my core I still felt as if His love toward me was conditional. That somehow, I needed to earn His love. What I know now is that it really boiled down to a trust thing. I loved God. I loved His son Jesus. I was filled with the Holy Spirit. And yet at the very core of my heart, I trusted no one, not even my Creator.

This is where I found myself as I sat in church on Mother's Day Sunday 1998. I was staring out at the others in the congregation as the pastor was handing out carnations to mothers. Pink ones for moms, red to grandmothers, and a few white ones to the great grandmothers in the room. I cheered and was happy to see my husband's mother get her pink carnation. I was even smiling and slightly giggled with the rest of the congregation as the pastor joked about not yet being able to give her a red one; although, inside my heart was breaking. I had avoided thinking about it for nearly two months and here it was slapping me in the face again. I was a failure. I couldn't produce a grandchild for our parents let alone an heir for my husband, the first-born son. I wanted a child. I wanted a family. I wanted the picture in my head. I managed to get through church without a tear falling, well, I may have wiped one or two while covering a fake cough. Finally, the service ended. I even managed to make it through the family dinner.

Afterward, though I found an excuse to get in my car and take a drive. The tears flowed uncontrollably then. It had been two months since the last appointment with the doctor and my body had done nothing since. I knew a decision had to made, for my own health reasons. It is not good for a woman's body to not do what it normally should. I knew when my husband got home I would have to discuss with him what to do. Once I was under control again, and I had stopped at a gas station bathroom to wash my face of tears, I returned home. That night John's response to my questions seemed so simple, logical, and absolute that I did not dare reveal my shaking insides. He said, "So first off, you take another pregnancy test just to be sure, then you call the doctor and do what she says, if that is to take the pills, then you take the pills."

It was a very restless night. I was up so many times. I knew I would do what my husband had said but I didn't want to. I didn't want to face another negative pregnancy test, yet another reminder of my failure. I was trying to plan the day, so I could do the test without anyone in the house knowing. It was such a small apartment. John's youngest brother still lived there as well as his mom and step dad, and we all shared one bathroom. How would I ever sneak enough alone time to take the test, plus deal with the onslaught of tears I knew would inevitably follow, plus a phone call to the doctor. Remember there were no cell phones at this time. Every phone call was right in the middle of the kitchen where the phone hung on the wall. No privacy at all. I had thought I would buy the test and take it with me to school and use the restroom there. As much as I hated this idea it seemed my only option.

John had left for work earlier so as I made my way to the kitchen for a quick breakfast before leaving to face my day. His mom was in the kitchen. I put on my cheery happy morning face as I greeted her. As I think on it now, it is a bit amazing how easily I could put that mask on and throw those walls up, but I had been doing it a very long time and was very good at it. She said she was glad she had caught me before I left as she wanted to ask me if I wanted to go to Wal-Mart with her and a friend this afternoon. They had planned to leave at a certain time but said that they could wait an extra thirty minutes for me to get home from class, if I wanted to go. I was almost instantly overjoyed, without giving away my secret happiness, I calmly stated I was so sorry I couldn't because after class I needed to go to the library to complete the research for my final paper. I did request that she say hello for me and encouraged her, they should stick to their plan, that it was so thoughtful of them to consider waiting on me.

I may need to explain something to you here. The closest Wal-Mart to where we were living at the time was a forty-five-minute drive. Any time someone was going to make the drive, you informed any and all that might need or want something or might even want to ride along. It's just what was done, whether you really wanted to or not, you just did. So either out of respect, or true desire they were asking me to go along, and I was pleased with the invitation. On any other day I would have graciously accepted. Not this day. I needed this day alone. Before I had even finished my answer in reply, I had already calculated out how much time I would actually have all to myself, alone in the apartment before anyone else would return home. So, yes, I admit I lied about going to the library. Later, I did ask the Lord and her for forgiveness.

I rushed out of class, I think before most of my classmates had even packed up their belongings. I raced home pushing the limits as far as I knew I could get away with. I stopped at the pharmacy for a pregnancy test and bought the cheapest one because I had already taken so many and spent enough money on the expensive ones just to throw them in the trash. I got to the apartment and was thrilled to see there really was no one there. I knew I had at least an hour maybe a bit longer all to myself. I marched in, threw my stuff in our little room, and headed straight for the bathroom. Now as I have stated before I had taken so many tests already that I knew the instructions by heart. I just tore open the box, took out the test and threw all the papers and instructions into the trash. Buried in the trash would be more of a correct statement. It was my thought no one would accidentally find it that way.

After taking the test I set it on the back of the toilet to wait the allotted three minutes, but I couldn't sit there. I fled from the room as if it were a hot oven. The emotions hit me like a boulder and I began praying and crying and begging God to help me to accept the outcome. I prayed I would be able to take the pills that the doctor would prescribe, that they would not affect me, like so many of the others had. I prayed that God would help me to be strong enough to not cry when I called the doctor, that I would accept the decision. Then I cried that my body was so horrid and mixed up and why could I do nothing right. I must have circled the kitchen table forty times while praying before I could bring myself to go look at the negative pregnancy test. It was definitely longer than three minutes anyway. As I walked the few short steps back to the bathroom I had convinced myself to just not even look at it, just throw it away. But look at it I did. I had to stare at it and figure out why it looked different then the last eleven I had taken. It had two little pink lines on it. One was faint but there were absolutely two.

I dug through the garbage so fast for those stupid instructions. I was sure I had done it wrong or perhaps because this was the cheap store brand it was different than the expensive ones I had taken before. Sure, enough one line equaled negative but two lines equaled positive. This stupid test was broken! It was saying I was pregnant and I knew that I wasn't! What should I do?

What I did next was not at all thought out. It was all instantaneous and unplanned. I ran to the kitchen phone pulled the phone book out and looked up the pharmacy phone number. I dialed the number. I asked to be transferred to a pharmacist. To my horror, a male pharmacist answered the phone. I hesitated only a moment, but my mouth kept moving. I explained that I had just come into the store and bought their store brand pregnancy test and had taken it. There were two pink lines on the test, could he please tell me what that means. (Oh, yes, I did…)

He may have been very shocked by my question, but he remained very professional and said, "Well, two lines means, you are pregnant." Without hesitation I replied, "Are you sure?" Then he very politely explained that their store brand tests had to be rigorously tested just as all the name brand tests had to be. They were clinically proven to be 99.8% accurate, that, the likelihood of a false negative was greater than a false positive. With this I paused a moment, trying to take it all in. Could this man really be telling me what I was so hopeful to hear? Was I dreaming? No, I was really standing here holding a positive pregnancy test in my hand. After a very long pause I said this, "What do I do now?" Feel free to laugh! I still do when I tell the story.

The next moment this amazingly gentle older man softened, the edge of professionalism leaving, and a hint of fatherly/grandfatherly love and maybe a bit of amusement, entered his tone and he replied, "If I were you, I would call a doctor, because you, my dear, are going to need a doctor." I am sure he was smiling. He probably even laughed out loud after I thanked him, and we hung up.

I stood there for a moment, one hand still on the phone as it hung on the wall and the other holding the pregnancy test, as the whole conversation unfolded again in my mind. Could it really be so? Is it true? I was so overwhelmed that I began to cry and laugh all at once. I skipped around the apartment and cried out my thanks to God. Maybe He really did care for me? Perhaps God really did care about the things that weren't sin and salvation related. Was it possible that He would do this for me just because He wanted to show His love for me? I was crying, singing and thanking God almost simultaneously. As I began to somewhat control myself, I found I was so excited I needed to tell someone.... But the problem was, there was no one home to tell! It was going to be a very long wait. In fact, I knew that the first person I needed to tell was my husband, but he would not be home from work for several hours. The first person to return home was John's youngest brother. Yep, he found out before my husband. I was just so elated.

Children of Healing

The Transition

I did make an appointment with the doctor and explained I was indeed pregnant. You see I was a nursing student with connections at the hospital lab. So, when I informed one of my friends at the hospital that I thought I was pregnant, she walked me straight to the lab and demanded a blood test to be sure. Yes, indeed! I was! The doctor was indifferent and scheduled an ultrasound to be sure. I think she perhaps felt a little bad about how our last encounter had gone down, but she was also admittedly dubious. Hence, the ultrasound before she even agreed to see me. The day of the ultrasound the technician was the same technician who diagnosed the Poly Cystic Ovary Syndrome. She flat out told me I was the last person on the planet she expected to see in here again for a prenatal exam. She said, "I saw those ovaries Honey, and I thought to myself 'poor thing.' But now here we are looking at a little tiny miracle, with a good strong heartbeat!" It was decided I was in fact eight weeks pregnant.

Taking those pictures home, I was on cloud nine! I couldn't wait to share what God had done! I took those ultrasound pictures everywhere I went and told just about anyone who would listen. The time came for me to graduate and take my state boards and then John and I headed to the west coast to start a new chapter in our lives, as a family, not just a couple.

It was a splendid trip! We took our time and made a vacation out of the drive, stopping at several places along the way that John had never seen. One of the highlights was spending the 4th of July in Washington DC. I have never been in such a sea of people in all my life. It was estimated that a million people were there that year to see the fireworks. It was crazy. It was amazing.

There were rows upon rows of porta-potties. I had never seen so many in one place before in my whole life. Being three months pregnant, you know I visited those a lot. The last time I visited them I had a very hard time relocating John and our place we had staked out on the grass. In fact, it was such a moment of panic, of being lost, yet knowing right where I was, that it is a moment permanently etched in my mind. It was quite a while until I finally located John. I had been gone so long even he was starting to worry.

The truth was, we both had started praying that I would get back soon. You see, John was starting to worry because I had been gone so long., while I was having an argument in my head. In my mind it felt silly that I was asking God to help me find my husband when

I knew right where he was, I just couldn't see him. I have come to learn that sometimes we can be so reliant on our own intelligence and be so confident in our own abilities that we forget to ask God for His help, or His opinion, or even His plan. For example, I have always been good at reading maps and making a plan. My dad taught us efficiency and critical thinking/problem solving skills. I had no reason to believe I would get lost walking to a row of porta-potties I had already visited many times that day. I knew we were by the only tree on the side of the Washington monument facing the Reflecting Pool and Lincoln Memorial. I was confident in my ability to return to that spot. What changed? The number of people in the area is what made the difference. No longer was just my husband near the only tree I could spot but he was joined by thousands of others. I knew right where he was and yet I could not find him in the massive sea of faces. It was like a *Where's Waldo* book page!

Have you gotten yourself into a place where you had all confidence when starting out and now you are completely lost? The situation changed as you were momentarily at a pit-stop? Even while you were doing the thing you needed to be doing? May I suggest you stop and ask God for help. Even if you started this process without consulting with Him first, it's never too late to invite Him back into it. When I stopped searching and bowed my head in a desperate prayer, the very first face I really focused on when I looked up again was the face of my husband. He was probably less than twenty-five yards from where I stood.

Watching the fireworks on such a grand scale and in our nation's capital, was one of the most amazing things to me. I sat on the grass and watched the big beautiful blooms of color exploding against the night sky. Feeling the concussion of them, nearly pushing me down against the ground, it is a memory that I cherish.

The pregnancy really was an easy one. Yes, there were moments of sickness, but I was just so excited it didn't really bother me. I did the things you are supposed to do and once we arrived in Washington State I did get established with another doctor. Nothing outstanding happened during this new visit other than listening to that little heartbeat. I cried. She checked me and did bloodwork and then scheduled an ultrasound at twenty weeks. We were very excited. She asked us if we wanted to know the sex of the baby. We weren't sure. We would discuss it and let them know at the next appointment, but we had names picked out already for either a boy or a girl.

I would learn many things about myself during this pregnancy. Up to this point in my life I had been told and raised to not show prejudice. That all people were created equal in God's eyes, and that He loved everyone. I was not raised to look at skin color or sex. I was taught to respect those in authority and my elders. I had always been a "good girl" so I never experienced any backlash or judgment for decisions because I was a rule follower, not a rule breaker. I will admit here though that I had little tolerance for those who did. Why was it so hard for them to just do the right thing?

However, at the time, I would tell you that I didn't judge anyone. I would say that everyone makes mistakes sometimes. I now know though, I have been guilty of wearing my own set of Pharisee robes in the form of pride. I may not have understood it as such back then, but it really does boil down to pride. When you think you are better than someone because you have not made the same mistakes they have made, it is pride. The Lord was going to make this very real to me.

I had no idea of the hidden judgements toward mistakes and poor decisions that I had inside. I did learn during this time in such a unique and clear way what judgmental glances can do. Also, how hurtful the just loud enough huffs and grunts of disapproval can be. You see, I have a very young-looking face, which I have been told I would appreciate it later in life, but as a teenager and young twenty something I couldn't wait to actually look older.

As a newlywed and college student, I finally agreed to my need for braces. I ended up wearing them for nearly three years. So, just imagine with me, a fourteen or fifteen-year-old girl, with sweet little freckles and braces. That would be me, but I was nearly twenty and had been married for over a year, pushing two! I soon learned, none of that mattered, at first impression. Imagine, that same little girl with freckles and braces; now add pregnancy to the picture. Does it change your view of that girl? Does her sweet little freckled face somehow turn into a mischievous troublemaker who probably deserved this? No? Well then think about this, when was the last time you saw a pregnant teen? What were your first thoughts? I bet they are different thoughts then if you had run into one of your married friends in the mall and discovered she was pregnant! You might do a little happy dance and squeal. There may even be lots of hugging and then maybe you might even rub her baby bump. I guarantee you, that is not what happens when people see a pregnant teenager! Because to most people who didn't know me, that is exactly what I looked like.

I don't think I could even begin to tell you the number of older women who looked at me with nothing but pure disgust on their faces. Oh, there were the occasional looks of sheer pity thrown in here and there, but mainly it was disgust and disapproval. I would get so frustrated at being treated like a second-class citizen, that I wanted to wave my hand in their faces, point to my wedding ring and scream this was here first and this child is a miracle gift from God. I may have done it once or twice, except I didn't scream, out loud anyway.

There were times that even others who knew me would notice the glances or hear the just under the breath comments. My mom would on occasion just start a conversation, out loud, with no one in particular, "Yes, Sissy, Daddy and I are so proud of you and John, how you have worked so hard to complete a nursing degree right out of high school and sticking to it, both of you finishing school. And look at you now: married almost two years and carrying my first grandbaby, which is just as amazing, since the doctor said you wouldn't! Yep, I guess I am one Blessed Momma!" Then she would rub my belly and say something like, "Baby, I don't know if you are a boy or a girl, but you are so loved and so wanted. We can't wait to meet you!" Then my Momma would give the sweetest smile to the one who had just given us a withering glare. Inevitably their faces and attitudes had changed, and they happily joined in her joy. To which she would then respond, "She may look young, but how many nineteen-year-old nurses do you know?" This would illicit a shocked, sheepish, shake of the head.

I became so broken for unwed teenage moms that I have tried ever since to initiate conversations. Ones without judgement or guilt. And also letting a teen mother know I see her for who she is and not the baby bump that protrudes in front of her. Just because most of us don't have our mistakes posted right out in front of us everywhere we go, does not give anyone the right to be instantly judgmental. Can you imagine how different the world would be if we were to wear our sins right out in the open for all to read? How sad is it that we think we can hide them and conceal them from our Loving Father God? To Him they are just as obvious as a protruding full-term baby belly. Time to look past people's outside, see their hurting faces, and love them with the love of Christ so that they will want to know Him too. I am thankful God can use everyday life things to teach us about the deep things of God.

I don't think I could possibly explain our excitement in the days leading up to the ultrasound. We vacillated back and forth over whether we wanted to know the sex of the baby. We did not need to know as we were very prepared already. You see we had been given a baby shower by our family and friends in New York before we moved to Washington. We had also saved up and bought a crib set I had fallen in love with during my last semester of school, in preparation for the future. I was not pregnant at the time, but we knew eventually we would use it. So, it was tucked away in the cedar chest along with the other things we had collected here and there, all in preparation for when we got our own place. So really it all boiled down to did we want to know? We decided that we did.

The News

Just a few weeks before the ultrasound we moved into our own apartment. For the first time in our married life we had our very own place. It was a cute little two-bedroom, one bath. We were finally able to pull out the majority of our wedding presents and the things we had purchased and stored away for the last two years. I was so happy. I was finally feeling like we were really starting our own life. I was beginning to be able to tell that ugly little voice in my head that it was wrong. I was making something of myself. I really was not a failure. I was a wife. I was a nurse. And now I was going to be a mom - even though the doctor said I wouldn't be. It didn't matter that John was still looking for a job, I knew God would provide; after all, He had already proved the doctor wrong! In the meantime, we were helping clean and paint apartments for the apartment complex we lived in. And hadn't that been Godly provision also! Of course, it was. Life was good.

It did not take any time at all to set up house in our little place and I do believe mom and I set up the baby's room first! While John spent half his time looking for a job and the other half his time finishing his correspondence classes in programing, I was busy dreaming about our baby and our life. I was so proud of John and also completely and utterly amazed that he would agree to move all the way across the country with me. A complete departure from his family's way of doing things. We began looking for a church to attend and had some sort of schedule. It included the cleaning of apartments, school, and job searching.

We were doing well. There were days that cleaning apartments was dreary. Mom, Dad and John all tried to get me to rest as often as I could, but I couldn't hardly sit and watch them all do the work. I felt I needed to help. The thoughts of going to work and using my nursing degree were constant; however, who was going to hire an obviously pregnant nurse? We needed God to provide. And indeed, He did, although not quite in the timing that I felt He should. I have heard it said many times that "God is the slowest to show up on time." For us at this time that was certainly true. In fact, when John brought home his first paycheck, a few weeks after the ultrasound, we were literally down to our last $8.32!

The morning of the ultrasound was an exciting one even with the talk at the breakfast table about my strange dream a few nights before. I had dreamed we went in to the scan and they took us straight to deliver the baby and John was calling his mom not to tell her the sex of the baby but telling her the baby was here. We had a laugh as we shared the silliness of the dream.

We left and arrived early for the appointment. We were sitting in the waiting room all smiles.

As we looked around the waiting room it became apparent we were the only excited ones in the room. There was an older woman in a wheelchair with multiple IV's. She looked as if the weight of the world rested on her bent shoulders. Next to us an older man with an ugly freshly stapled incision right down his whole chest, I'm sure, but only a few inches of it showed above the neck of his hospital gown. It appeared to be his daughter next to him. There was another couple in the room across from us as well.

My pregnant belly made the nature of our appointment about as obvious as the medical scars and equipment in the room made their reasons obviously not as joyous as ours. As I surveyed the room my mom let out a bit of a stifled laugh. The woman next to her dad asked, "Are you here to find out the sex of the baby?"

"Oh YES! This is my first grandbaby!" she practically squealed. "But I was just thinking about the sermon we heard Sunday and it made me think how Blessed we are to even be sitting here. You see this baby, according to one doctor was never supposed to be! But God had other plans." And then my mother proceeded to repeat the Sunday message right there in the waiting room. I believe that God meant for her to do so because for those precious minutes not a single person was called to leave the room. It was as if we were all in a protected bubble of time.

My mind recalled the events of just three days before. We were all sitting in church listening to a special guest speaker. He said he was going to preach on a very familiar story. One he was sure we had all read and heard before, but that he hoped we would see it through new eyes. You know this story. It's the one where Jesus falls asleep on the boat and a huge storm comes and all the disciples panic and wake him up saying, don't you care that we are going to die? Then, of course Jesus rebukes the storm and the disciples stand all amazed and wondering who this really is that even the weather obeys Him. Remember that one? Sure, we have all heard it before. But then the pastor got very excited saying, "I want to show you something that maybe you didn't notice before. You can read this story in three of the Gospels, but in Mark and Luke you see that Jesus said to the disciples when they were getting into the boat. 'Let's go over to the other side,'."

When the storm started raging and they started to panic, not one of them remembered the words Jesus had said. He already said they were going over to the other side. They *would* end up over there. Then the pastor said, "I know there are some of you facing major storms in your life right now. You may even think Jesus fell asleep and has no idea what you are facing. Let me just say to you, have you forgotten the words Jesus said, 'I will never leave you or forsake you.' Have you forgotten He said He would be with us in all times of trouble, that when we call upon His name there He is? Jesus told them, they were going to end up on the other side. You *are* going to the other side even though the storm is raging. Remember what Jesus said!" Then the pastor had everyone go home and write down the top three things they needed from God today. He said bring them back tonight. We are going to lay them on this altar pray over them and remember God is who He says, and He said we are going to the other side. We had brought back our list that night. It only contained these two things, a healthy baby and a job.

As I listened to my mom repeat the sermon, I began to rub my belly. This was the child that was never to be. This was a promise. This was the other side. I recalled the worship that night as so many were all down around the altar. I had felt the baby move very dramatically and it caught my breath. I was in the middle of worship with my hands in the air. I responded instantly to the movement by putting my hand on my belly and half laughing said, "That's right baby, that's what it feels like to be in the presence of the Lord." What a sweet memory and I couldn't help smiling. As I was pulled out of my thoughts, I looked again around the room as my mom finished with a mini altar call of her own saying to everyone, "... so I know that whatever it is that has brought you all in here today, God wants you to know He loves you and He said you were going to the other side." Faces, that minutes earlier were weary and downcast, now had smiles and a dramatically different countenance. And right then, we were called to go back for our appointment. Everyone waved and smiled and said good luck and a few said, "Thank you, thank you so much."

When we got back into the room with the technician there was great excitement and the usual assurance from the technician. She would do her best to tell us the sex of the baby, but she could make no promises. We assured her we understood. As she began the scan she was talking and smiling and then she became quiet and for a few moments there was a silence. John told me later it was an awkward silence on her part but that I was so excited I didn't notice. Regardless, it didn't seem long until she said, "If you will excuse me for a second, I seem to need some help here." I assumed the machine was giving her a problem. We visited a bit as we waited. I could not see the screen from where I was lying but John could. Another person came into the room and I seem to remember saying something like, "Is everything ok?" and he said, "Well I don't know. We are about to find out." This was my first indication that perhaps something was not right. The mood in the room instantly changed.

There was silence as he turned back on the machine and began to look. It did not seem to take him long. He shut the machine down wiped off my belly and helped me to sit up. He became what I would call very clinical. Professional, but very clinical and almost unfeeling. He explained that the other woman had left to come and get him to confirm her findings. That there was at this time "no fetal heart tones." My nursing brain began trying to translate his clinical speak.... *Wait he is saying there is no heartbeat.* As best as I could I spoke out loud, "So you are telling me there is no heartbeat. The baby is…. dead." This last part came out in almost a whisper.

Yes, that is what this man was trying to tell me. I think he said some more words, but I don't remember what they were. All the thoughts in my head began screaming at each other so loud I heard nothing else. *This can't be true. Make him do it again. Two people checked you idiot they both saw the same thing. But this was our miracle baby. God changed His mind. You can't be a mom. You failed again. But I wanted to be one. He proved the doctor wrong. He could do it again.* All this and so much more began waging an instant war in my head. He stepped out of the room saying someone else would be in momentarily. As he pulled the door closed my eyes came up to meet the eyes of my husband. The very first words to come from anyone's mouth were his. He said this, "We ARE going to the other side." And then he was instantly up out of his seat with his arms around me and we cried together.

The nurse part of my brain would not let me sit and cry for very long, I began trying to figure out what would happen next. I needed a plan. I have never liked being startled or caught off guard, somehow by knowing ahead of time what to expect I could in my mind take back control of the situation. I knew how far along in the pregnancy that I was, so I could only come up with two possibilities. I immediately knew my decision - *but would my family agree with me?* I desperately needed them too. I sat back from John and said, "I think I know what they are going to say. I think I have two options and I know which one I want to choose." He was at first shocked by my choice but then when I explained he also agreed. Secretly, I think, we both wished for another option; but there was not one. I explained the options and my choice to my mom, when she returned. She had stepped out of the room, so as not to fall apart in front of us and also to give us some time.

Soon the door was knocked on and someone else entered again. This time we were introduced to Sue. She was a certified nurse midwife and she was here to explain what would happen next. She at least had an edge of compassion that was obvious to me and even though she was very professional, she cared. She began to repeat the "because of no fetal heart tones..." I at this point interrupted her... "You can say the baby has no heartbeat. We believe it's a baby not just a fetus."

With a half-smile and the nod of her head she quietly said, "Me too." She informed us that I indeed had two choices and proceeded to tell my family almost word for word what I had already told them. Option A would be a D&C, the room had already been notified and was on stand-by. I could be in and out in under an hour and probably wouldn't even need to stay overnight. Option B was to induce labor and go through the birth.

She had barely finished her sentence and had not even taken a breath when I said, "Labor, I choose labor." She tried to hide her surprise.

My mom was the first to explain. "She is a nurse and quite honestly she just sat here and told us what you were going to say before you came in here and said it. Honestly, I am amazed that she was so right on. Her concern is that a D&C is too much like an abortion to her and that it will tear apart the baby. Is that so?" At this comment Sue looked from me to my mom to me again. In answer to mom's question she hung her head an almost speaking to the floor said, "Yes, that's true."

I did know that, but I think my family needed the confirmation of it. Finally, I said, "I have carried this baby so long and desired it for so long that I need to see it, I need to hold it. Do you understand that? Is that ok?"

At this point she walked over laid her hand on my arm and said, "Yes I do. It is your right as a mom to hold your baby." She did caution us that because we didn't know what went wrong the baby may not be...normal. I assured her it didn't matter. I needed to do it this way. She left to set it all up.

It took quite a while for her to return. It seems I had not made the popular choice. Many in the hospital would rather I just get in and get out. Sue became the best advocate for me, I pray many blessings on her for it to this day. She returned telling us the maternity floor was full and they did not have an opening for me until three days from now. Or the option for a D&C still existed. "Fine, I will go home and be back in three days," I declared. But inside I cried out to God how could I go home and wait that long knowing things were not ok.

When we returned to the apartments, my mom went to tell my dad. John was indeed having to call his mom and tell her the baby was coming just not how we expected it too… As the phone was still ringing in his hand, I needed solace. I headed to our room and shut the door very hard. For the first time all day I was instantly and intensely angry. I balled up my fists up in the air and wanted to just pummel my belly but as my arms came down I pounded them into the pillow as hard as I could then I threw myself face down on the bed. Waves of salty hot tears soaked my pillow. Why was this happening? What had I done wrong? God, I tried so hard to do all the right things? Why was I not good enough? Was it all some mean trick? Sobs from so deep down poured forth so violently my body shook and ached all at the same time.

I don't know how long I laid there. I do recall having to talk on the phone to Tony. She was a new acquaintance who would become a friend. We had met just the day before. She was heartbroken with us and told us we were in her prayers. The fact that she cared enough to call and check on us and how the appointment went meant so much. Even though it didn't go how any of us expected.

Mom and Dad walked over. Dad could not speak. It was obvious all of us had been crying, he just grabbed me and held on very tight, then John, then me again. When the room was somewhat composed we explained the events as they had unfolded and how we were going to go back in three days. As we talked the phone rang, John answered it. As I kept explaining the process, we heard him get louder and he said, "Just a minute I will ask her." He put his hand over the receiver, it was the hospital. "They have found us an opening if we can be there in two hours they will start the induction." I nearly jumped off the couch, "We'll be there! I can pack a bag in 10 minutes." We all thanked God that we did not have to wait the three long days.

Children of Healing

The Day

Once we arrived at the hospital we were taken to the opposite side of the maternity ward, there would be no other new moms around or cries of new babies to make this any harder. It seemed very sad and yet very considerate at the same time. Our nurse was cordial but subdued. Sue met us almost immediately. We thanked her so much as the nurse had made it clear she was the one who had pushed so hard to get us in today. She also indulged us and had a portable ultrasound machine brought in for one more "just in case maybe we are wrong" look. My mom pushed for this knowing that God could change the situation, even now, by performing a miracle.

This time Sue walked us step by step through the scan pointing out the baby and what we should see and what she couldn't see and what might cause concern for when baby arrived. We thanked the tech and her for one last hopeful look. Then after I was sufficiently hooked up with IV's she began the induction. She explained because this was my first baby, labor could go on well into the next day. It would all depend on how my body reacted to all of this. My blood pressure was sky high, so I was given medicine for that. I was also given a morphine pump to regulate my pain because at this point they were not concerned with the medicine passing to the baby only my comfort. "Honestly if you could rest it would be best," she said. She assured us she would be back in bit.

We tried to talk or play cards anything to pass the time, but it became apparent pretty quickly the medicine was making me nauseous. My poor nurses, I kept apologizing to them because they ended up having to change my sheets. I felt horrible, like I was being an extra burden. They assured me this was quite a normal response to the medication. Mom and Dad who had not eaten much all day decided to go find some food and bring some back for John too. I was so thankful that he never left my side.

It was during this time our nurse showed up and said our Pastor was here to visit. John and I were shocked, how did he know and why did he come? I mean after all we had only been attending the church about a month! But in walked Pastor D, the Associate Pastor of our new church. He explained that Mom had called the church office asking for prayer for us. He said he knew he needed to come and pray with us. The fact that he came touched such a soft spot in my heart that I could almost believe God did not mean for me to suffer through this. I began thinking that God really did care about me and He needed me to know I was not alone. We filled Pastor in on the process and then he prayed with us, hugging us both and telling us he would still be praying.

About four hours into the induction, or about midnight, Sue and the nurse returned to check on the progress. She was pleased with the progress and quite surprised. I was one hundred percent effaced and four centimeters dilated. I knew God was answering prayers. I did not want to have to be there "well into the next day." Sue explained that her shift was ending but that she was not leaving me or handing me over to someone else. She would stay until the baby was born. She was going to lay down in one of the extra rooms and if I needed anything the nurse would get her. I was so moved by this I could not speak, tears just poured down the side of my face.

During much of this time John thought I was sleeping because I had my eyes closed and I had been instructed to rest. The truth was though that I needed to block out much of the world around me. I was not asleep but praying and begging God to help me through this. Everything hurt, every cell in my body ached and even my soul ached. I don't think there are words to describe the hollow emptiness that I felt. As I laid there so many thoughts tumbled through my brain. *What had I done wrong? Did I get into a chemical? Did I move wrong? Had I done something to hurt the baby even before I knew I was pregnant? Had I sinned? Was this a punishment? Was God really angry with me? Did I deserve this? Was this more proof that I didn't measure up? How could I do this? Would the baby be deformed? What if this didn't work would they still make me do the D&C?* It seemed there was a never-ending barrage of incomplete thoughts. And I was desperately trying to shut them up.

A few hours later I stirred on the bed and with help walked to the bathroom again only to realize this was not what I needed, Mom realized it immediately too and helped hurry me back to the bed. Telling Dad and John the baby was coming. Dad was out the door like a shot to find someone and John was pushing the call bell. I barely made it back on the bed when the baby arrived. It was as if we all froze not knowing what to do. Sue arrived very quickly and went to work. I asked, "What is it?" She didn't know yet. The baby had been born still completely in the amniotic sac. It was not until she opened the sac that she declared, "It's a girl!"

"Her name is Hannah." I said, "Hannah Christine."

Sue gently picked her up and laid her in the blanket we had brought with us. She was so tiny and yet so perfect. John's words later described that moment so well, "She looked as if you could do CPR on her little body that she would be fine." We admired the details of her little bitty body. Her long little legs. John's mom's chin. The delicate little fingers, all ten of them, and all ten tiny little toes. Later we would find out she weighed in at about twelve ounces. She was so precious and so little even the nurse was amazed at her.

John took her and held her then, as Sue needed to finish with me. There were some complications and issues with the rest of the birth that she needed my full attention and I needed hers. She was at first apprehensive to share all the details, but I needed to see, to be involved. She understood. It was partly during this time that we began to piece some of the puzzle together and begin to understand some of why this happened. In short, the placenta and umbilical cord both had issues and had not grown like they should. Because of the nature of the issues when she got bigger and demanded more nutrients she could not get what she needed. When Sue felt as if I was stable enough for her to leave us alone she gave us some brief instructions, hugged me, and left.

The next several moments are permanently ingrained in my mind. I watched my husband rocking his first born and singing "Jesus loves me... this I know... for the Bible... tells me so..." as tears just ran down his face. He looked at her like every new dad looks at his child, in complete awe and amazement, along with the tears that showed the pain of saying hello and goodbye in the same meeting. To this day and even as I type this, the tears still flow thinking about this tender moment.

Perhaps it is a tradition in your family, like it is in ours, to take your children to the church and publicly dedicate them to the Lord. It should seem obvious to you that we were not going to get that opportunity with Hannah; however; at that moment it seemed like the most important and appropriate thing for us to do. To give her back to the Lord since He was the one who gave her to us. We asked my dad to do it, to be the one to pray. It was very difficult for him. Dad does not do hospitals very well and he doesn't do funerals well either. He could not look at her and I knew this before she was born. I was not hurt or offended by this. I love my dad and knew his feelings about it. I did ask him for this though. So, he very gently accepted the little white blanket burrito in which she lay all covered. He began perhaps one of the hardest prayers he has ever prayed. In that one simple yet incredibly important prayer we accepted with grace, dedicated with thanksgiving, and said with hearts full of love good bye to our precious little girl. We gave her back to the Lord - who had given her to us.

I feel that it is necessary to step aside again for a moment to address something very important. Perhaps you are reading this book because you know me, and you were purely curious. Perhaps you are reading it because someone suggested that you should or maybe you picked it up by merely a whim. Whatever the reason you find yourself reading this, there may be a nagging question in your brain right now. Why? Why do you want to remember this? Why record such a sad story? Let me remind you of another story. It is recorded in the book of Acts and it finds Paul and Silas weary and beaten. I guarantee they had not planned that morning to end up sitting chained together bleeding and sore. If we walked in on that story and it only stopped there, where would the hope be?

But the good news is the story doesn't stop there! Paul and Silas began to praise the Lord. I wonder if, like my husband, as they started to sing did it come out shaky and still with tears running down their faces. I wonder did it hurt to take the next breath just to sing the next line of the song. I do think however, as they began to sing their voices began to get stronger, just like my daddy's as he thanked God for such a tiny precious little girl whose heart no longer beat. For Paul and Silas as their voices got stronger the earth began to quiver. I think that as the singing, in pure heartbroken openness reached the throne of God, He began to tap his feet. As the praise began to increase and they no longer noticed the stabbing pain of the next breath they began to shout their songs of worship. In my mind's eye the Lord could no longer contain it, He jumped to His feet with thunderous applause causing the Earth to tremble so violently that the chains in that prison cell shattered as the gates flung wide open.

God took what was undeniably one of Paul and Silas's worst days and turned it into one of the recordable moments in His book. If God can step into that dark, damp, pain infested basement prison then He can certainly step into ours. God wants us to know that He has the ability to take what may be one of our worst, most unplanned messes and turn it around! He can shatter chains and bust open those walls that hold us captive even if it means He has to rip open the earth to do it! All that He desires is for us, His kids, to give to Him our whole heart. Did you catch that? Our WHOLE heart. But He doesn't even require that it be all in one piece as long as we hand it all over to Him. One of the greatest things of all about this amazing, chain shattering, gate crushing, Earth ripping God, is that He is the ultimate gentleman! Not once, **Not Ever**, will He force you to give it to Him. He will not ever override your will to give those secret locked up parts of your broken heart to Him. Don't misunderstand me… He wants them. He desires them, He wants more than anything for you to allow Him to take them, mend them, create in you a new heart and set it free. But He WILL NOT demand them. He will sit patiently at the door of your heart, waiting for the words He longs to hear. Here you go Father, it isn't much, but it is all I have, you can have it.

I tell you my story in hopes that as you read it, you will begin to understand more clearly just how great, is the love, the Father has for us. Just how patient He can be with His children. I wish that I could tell you that in that hospital room the earth shook, the air came back to my daughter's lungs and we all went home and lived happily ever after. The story doesn't go that way. But if you will keep reading you will find that God had His hand on it. That He wrote the ending. That my story isn't over yet, and neither is yours! Hang in there, God is listening for the hearts of His children when they cry out to Him. Sometimes we have gone very far and think He cannot possibly remember the sound of our voice. I assure you that no matter where you are today, what you have done, whatever prison you find yourself locked away in, He can hear you and He is waiting on the edge of His seat to bust in there and change the ending of the story.

The Aftermath

I know that I did not sleep much that night in that uncomfortable hospital bed. I cried. I hurt. I wanted the world to end. I began to doubt all the truth I had been telling people about how this pregnancy was miraculous. Isn't that just like the enemy to sneak in when you are down and wounded and continue to whisper his lies in your ear? Oh, and he knew what lies I would swallow, hook, line and sinker. He dove head long into his torment, saying that I was not good enough, God did not mean for me to ever have a family of my own, that I was indeed a failure. I wish I could tell you I was strong enough then to tell that sneaky snake where to go with his lies but I wasn't, not yet.

There were a few more complications during the night that required the nurses. At one point they considered the possibility that I may have to stay longer if the bleeding did not come under control. At that point I cried out to God, yet again, begging Him to intervene so I could go home and grieve in the privacy of my own home. He did. The bleeding stopped and did not start again. By morning I was exhausted and bone weary. I was relieved when we were told we could go home that afternoon. John called my parents to have them pick us up as he had stayed the whole night with me.

There were several "housekeeping" items that we had to do with the hospital that morning. One of which was they were required to send the social worker to talk to us. From the moment she set foot in our room it was awkward. It seemed very obvious to us she could not relate or didn't even know how to approach us. She gave us a canned speech about loss and the need to get involved in a support group even giving us the statistic of marriages that fail after the loss of a child. Seriously, she did! I remember feeling like I just wanted her to shut up and leave. I know she was only doing her job, but I felt as if she had as much compassion for me as stone.

I feel prompted to state here that if you are dealing with a loss and it is affecting your relationship you must know this important fact, men and women grieve differently! We would very soon discover this.

Immediately after the social worker left us we were once again surprised by the nurse telling us that our Pastor had returned. As much as the social worker had sucked all the air out of the room, when Pastor walked in so did a breath of fresh air. Compassion and love returned to the room as he hugged us both and cried and rejoiced at our announcement of the birth of our daughter. He prayed over us yet again, and we knew he cared and was seeking God on our behalf. Thanking God for His miraculous intervention in the whole birth process and the beautiful gift of a baby girl and then he prayed for God to mend the brokenness as we moved into tomorrow and the days ahead, even asking for children in the future when we were ready for them. By the time he left even though I still hurt I felt that God had not left us there alone.

When all paperwork and instructions had been given we were presented with a gift and card signed by all our nursing staff. Our short stay had impacted all the staff even the ones not directly working with us. I have learned over the years that God uses even strangers to teach us, to bless us, to reveal more of Himself to us. My prayer is that He used us for many of them that night.

During much of the morning though, it was a constant battle. There were tears that I could not control and there were many I fought back. I knew I could not fall all apart in this public place and the Lord gave me the grace that I needed to get through. So, by the time I was finally released to go home I was exceedingly grateful.

There was one more rather important moment that I feel I need to share with you which happened in the hospital. It happened just moments before we left. All the discharge papers were signed I was sitting in the wheelchair waiting for my dad to get the car. Mom had left with him and it seemed to be taking a while so John stepped out the door to see if he could see them. For the first time since entering the hospital I found myself completely alone.

I was sitting in the airlock between the double doors going into the hospital and the double doors going out to the parking lot. I was overwhelmed with emotion. I really felt like screaming. This would have been a very out of character thing for me to do. I was instantly angry and hurting so badly as if my insides were being shredded. All at once my arms physically ached and there was not breath in my lungs. I was getting ready to leave this hospital... *without my baby*. I wrapped my arms around myself and I am sure I would have collapsed to the ground had I not been sitting. Every bit of strength was gone as I screamed out loud in my head "*Oh God, Oh God*" while at the same time biting my tongue to keep from screaming it out loud. For as much as I loved Him and knew in my head He said He wouldn't leave me, I was also very angry and confused at why He would allow this to happen. And then just as quickly there was guilt for even considering being mad at God. I was a mess, I knew it, yet all I could do was simply scream His name. No other words would do.

When we were finally delivered to our apartment and my parents were sure we had no immediate needs, we both collapsed into bed in utter exhaustion. I have no idea how long we slept. I have no idea how many times I cried. I remember the pillow being soaked and I recall waking up with John's arm around me and briefly processing that I must have been crying in my sleep. The next several days are very hazy. I had a minor complication that momentarily caused my nurse brain to take over and handle, including calling the nurse on call and explaining the situation and we agreed I acted swiftly and correctly, agreeing if it happened again then they wanted to see me right away but if not to continue with the scheduled appointment.

There were several calls and cards from family and friends over the next several days and weeks. In truth I cannot recall how many reached out to us in this way. I know that I appreciated them all, but two of them stand out the most, a phone call from my aunt and the meeting with the Senior Pastor of our church.

The phone call with my aunt came almost immediately after returning home and then again, a few days later to check on me. I will never forget these words and have, in fact, repeated them to others often. "Karrie Ann, God is BIG enough for your anger." She gave me permission to be angry! I'm not sure if at any point in my life until then, was that ever an acceptable thought. That I could yell and scream at God all I wanted. He was big enough for it. The key though she cautioned was this, "Scream... cry... yell... whatever you need to do. JUST DON'T STOP TALKING TO HIM! Don't stop Karrie! Tell Him everything, in every moment. Whatever it is! He loves you. HE LOVES YOU. He... loves... you! He can handle whatever it is you need to say to Him."

How freeing it was for me to realize I could be honest with God in that way. Because the truth was, I had those things to say! I felt them bubbling deep inside me and if I didn't find a way to let them out I would self-implode. I am willing to bet you have felt that way sometime. But guess what? God is BIG enough for your anger too. He is not angry with us when we have emotional outbursts with Him. He does not shake His finger at us and say, "No, No, No, you can't talk like that." Instead He lifts us like the wounded child we are hugs us tightly and says, "I know, I know you hurt, I know you're mad and upset and I Still Love You." **Then** when we are ready to hear it, He says, "And I have a plan. This isn't the end of the story. It is all going to work out for your good, I promise. Just Trust Me with it. Trust me with your anger, Trust Me with your hurt. Trust Me."

Sometimes we don't trust God enough yet to hear Him talk about the plan He has. We are still too angry to trust yet, or still afraid. We need to learn to trust Him with our pain before we are ready to hear the rest. Sometimes He has to wait for us to stop yelling or for others it is to stop running, so that we can hear Him properly. There is a popular saying that says: 'Sometimes God calms the storm for His child, and sometimes He calms the child in the storm.' Have a conversation with Him today if you are confused as to which one applies to you this day.

Our daughter was born September 3rd. I know for a fact that we had Thanksgiving and Christmas that year, but I can't give you many details. I know my parents built a house during that time, but I don't have many memories of it. In fact, I have seen the pictures with me in them and I don't even remember the day or the experience. I was still grieving and probably dealing with some depression. I had no desire to get out of bed and when I did, nothing sounded good, nothing I did caused me pleasure or pain. If I wasn't crying, then I was numb. I got up and did the motions of the day, even church on Sundays. I even put on the smile and told the world I was doing OK. But inside that was so far from the truth.

I can recall one day after getting up and getting my husband out the door for work I was walking back to my room to get dressed for the day and walked past the door to the room that would have been the baby's room and fell into a heap there in the hallway and cried and cried. I lay on the floor for hours crying. I should also add praying, but the truth is closer to this, that I did more screaming and crying out to God from my brokenness then I did any listening. Many hours later I knew I needed to get up because my husband would be coming home and need dinner. I got out of the shower and was just barely dressed when he came home from work.

It was not long after that day I felt like either God said it or I just felt it, but this was enough. I needed to get back out and live life or I would not. I knew I needed something, so one day I got dressed and because I had no car, walked two blocks down the street to a nursing home and asked if they needed a nurse. I filled out the application and walked home. I got there just as the phone was ringing; they were calling me for an interview. I walked back an hour or so later and had a job before my husband came home from work! I don't know if it surprised him more that I was hired or that I actually went out looking for one that day, without any warning. His face was priceless and for the first time in a while I felt pure pleasure at his reaction.

Now I need to return to the second stand out conversation after we returned home. Did you think I forgot? I said there were two that stand out. Well, I didn't forget but the truth is, it applied even more as I got out of the apartment and started interacting with people again. To some degree it did before I got a job but more so as I was out and about and having conversations again. It was a meeting with the Senior Pastor of our church. He called John and I to come in and meet with him. I admit I was sort of apprehensive because, as you recall we had only been attending the church a short time and he was not the Pastor who came to the hospital to see us.

When we arrived at his office he was so warm and friendly it made us feel welcomed right away. He led us to a small sitting area in his office and sat down there with us not behind his desk. He stated he was sorry that he could not come to the hospital as he had been out of town but was informed of the happenings as soon as he was back. We assured him that Pastor D, who had arrived, was such a blessing to us and gave a brief account of the hospital social worker visit just moments before his return visit. It was this that lead him into his reason for calling us. He explained some of his grief process with us about losing his wife to cancer not two years earlier. Other than being told by someone at the church that the Senior Pastor's new wife was not his first wife we knew nothing of the story.

He said some things I was shocked to hear him say and yet they ministered deeply to me over the next year. He told us no one can tell you how to grieve. There is no rule book for it. And unfortunately, even those we love and even well-meaning Christian friends will do their best to comfort you. But people will say the wrong things, even dumb things. They don't mean it, but they don't know what else to say. They will tell you their stories of loss and that they understand how you feel. They don't. But they don't know what else to say. They will quote scripture at you until you want to throw the Bible at them. They don't know that all you need them to do is be there, to just say they are sorry and not try to make it all better; because they can't. Only God can do that, and it will take time.

This whole next year things will be tough. You will hit holidays and milestones and think of her. You will cry a lot and you will need to let each other cry. There is NO WRONG way to walk through this process because it's your process. Not mine. Not anyone else's. Yours. And if you need me, I'm here to listen. It was surprising short and refreshingly honest. He even said, "If you had come to me for counseling before my wife had died I had this great speech which I have given lots of times until I realized after she was gone that nothing I said to countless others, would have comforted me when she died. I knew all the right things to say and yet it didn't help the way I felt. Only God will heal those parts of you. You know Him, you know His word and He will walk you through this." Then he prayed for us a beautiful heartfelt prayer that only one whose heart had been broken and then restored could pray and then he hugged us both and we left.

We would soon discover the truth in his words as phone calls and cards came. Then there were the conversations with having to tell people, such as the clinic and the WIC meeting and those around us at church who knew we were pregnant and then suddenly not but had no baby with us. Those were hard days.

You may not understand some of these things I have said. Or maybe you are even guilty of saying some of the silly things we say when we are trying to comfort people, but instead we end up not helping at all. If your very next question to me is, "Well then what do I say?" Let me share a very tender moment that may help you. After we left the hospital the next several days we were just trying to survive the long hours of the day. My brother and his beautiful wife drove three hours south to be with us. After all the talking and "filling in" conversations had happened there were several moments of awkward silence. We tried to fill the time with playing cards or watching a movie.

It was while we were watching a movie at my parents' apartment that I was overcome with emotion again and instead of showing it I got up and walked to the bathroom. I left the lights off and cried silently trying to will the tears to stop flowing because I didn't want to make a scene. It was here my brother found me sitting on the closed toilet seat, crying, in the dark. He stepped out as if he was startled to see me there and I quickly got up thinking he might need to use the bathroom. As I took a step toward the door he stepped back in. It had occurred to him what was happening, and he had come back. As I nearly collided with him I was again overwhelmed with emotion that he came back. He put his great big strong Army Ranger arms around me and held me tight. Standing there in the dark neither of us said a word as he hugged me like when we were kids and I just cried. It may have been minutes or nearly an hour we stood there, I don't even know. When I was under control again I wiped my tears and the moment was over. We returned to the living room with everyone else and never spoke a word. To this day I don't think we have talked about that moment, but it is one of my most treasured, precious memories.

There is power in silence. There is power in just "being." If you don't know what to say, then don't say - Be. Be available. Be there to listen when they are ready to talk. Be there in their silence and understand the power of a hug, or even just sitting in a room. Perhaps each of you holding a cup of coffee that you don't ever drink, but somehow just that strengthens them, simply because it's shared. Learn to be comfortable in the uncomfortableness of someone else. Sometimes your presence is comfort enough.

Children of Healing

The Dream

Our church had small home groups and we had been invited to one which honestly, we had thought about attending even before the birth. On our first Sunday back, we found ourselves drawn to the couple whose home it was in and we were soon accepting the invitation to come that week. On the day of home group, we entered into the most inviting and comfortable place and it dispelled any doubts we may have had about coming. We were introduced as, "the couple they had prayed for last week who had just lost their child." This group loved us instantly and we knew it. During praise and worship we were broken, they all gathered around us and prayed for us nearly the entire hour. I think I was hugged by every woman there that night multiple times. We returned every week over the next year as they became very good friends.

● ● ●

It was here at home group where the Lord began another part of my healing. About three weeks after our first visit to our new home group one woman, whom I immediately connected with, pulled me aside and apologized saying, "I have to tell you something." I could tell she had been crying. I was very confused by the way this was all starting out, but she seemed so purposeful that I knew this was important. I remained still while she continued to speak. "A few weeks back I had the most amazing dream, it was so real," she said. She explained that she had seen a huge lion. Like the one seen in a popular painting with the Lion of Judah, the nail scars in his paws and the crown on his head and the key around his neck." I confirmed I knew of the picture of which she spoke. She continued. "He was so real and so big and amazing, and I was amazed to see he was playing with a little girl. It was as if they were playing tag and chasing each other. Running into the ocean waves on a beach and then running away from them as they came onshore. Then they were running through a field and the lion caught her and they tumbled to the ground laughing and enjoying each other's company. In fact, the lion reached over with his giant paw and embraced the child as in a hug and then gave her a sloppy wet kiss with his tongue. The child laughed with glee. She said by the sight of them they both were very happy." She said that then she woke up. "It was so amazing!" she said, "So real!" She had asked the Lord, "Wow God was that you and me?" She teared up and explained God had told her... "no." Her faced changed and she got quiet for a

minute. Nearly whispering she said, "It bothered me…
for several days it bugged me…"

"Several days later I was here for home group and
I thought about it again and asked again, 'Lord isn't that
me?' And again, He replied, 'No.' finally, almost
desperate, I said, 'Well then who is it?' just then I looked
up and I saw you walk in the door. It was your first time
here. I didn't know who you were. It was then the Lord
spoke to me so clearly, as I watched you walk in, 'It is
that woman's child.' I didn't know that you were the
couple whose child had just died until it was said later
on. Please forgive me - I just couldn't tell you that night.
I am so sorry that I didn't tell you sooner."

Of course, by this time we were both in tears.
Isn't God so amazing? In a time when I was so hurt, and
so broken God knew that I could probably not handle a
dream with my daughter in it. I would most likely go to
bed and not ever want to get up again. So instead He
gave the dream to someone else. Someone who would
be able to share it with me in such a way, that I really
could see it play out in my mind's eye. Not only that, but
He gave it to a complete stranger who would become a
dear friend at a time when I desperately needed one.

God is like that. He cares so deeply for us that he
will bring people into our lives for a reason, a season, or
a lifetime. Sometimes people will come into our lives and
stay, other times they come for only a moment. Just
because some of these friendships are only for a short
time, does not mean they are any less important or that
they were merely coincidental. God will use anyone to

• • •
61

speak into our life when we need it. Even if we don't think we need it. Ask Him to show you any of these "forgotten friendships" that He has used to speak to you in a moment of need or a moment of weakness or shame or fear. I pray even now He shows you times in which He placed people in your path or in your life as an agent for Him.

Perhaps today you need to take a moment and write down a list of people who you could thank the Lord for: that nurse at the hospital, that teacher who listened, that checker at the grocery store who smiles every time they see you, that lab partner in summer school, the supervisor who encouraged you to pursue your dream. Some of these people we may only share a very small fraction of our life with and yet God has used them to teach us, to grow us, to encourage us, to touch our lives in such a way that we are never the same. *Thank you, Lord, for the blessing of short term associations that inspired long term change in me and gave me a deeper understanding of who You are and how You see me.*

At that time in my life it brought me great comfort thinking about the dream of hers. I knew my daughter was in heaven but somehow the confirmation of someone else seeing her there made it more so. Giving validation to my belief and also let me know that just maybe even if God wasn't happy with me somehow because of my failures that at least He wasn't going to take it out on my daughter. For some that will sound like a strange statement and others will understand it completely.

I feel as though it is important to say something here, just because you see the outside of a person does not mean you know the inside. We all have seen those, who we think have it all together and seem so purposeful and confident only to hear them say later how frightened and unsure they were. Or we have even witnessed an event or situation that we thought someone handled beautifully to hear them later say how badly they had done and felt as if the whole thing was a failure. Look at the many lives lost, that the world found out much too late just how sad and broken their lives were and yet they hid behind a mask. Many have been celebrities and comedians, who we all thought had the perfect life. Yet it was just a mask, one they wore daily. May I just say, I had a great mask. I wore it so well that there were days that only God himself knew I was wearing it.

I guarantee there are many people around you every day, wearing a mask. They have a need to hide the shame, hide the hurt, hide the disappointment. They need the world to believe they have it together that they got this. Maybe you are the one in the mask. Maybe you walk around making people believe you are confident, when in truth you are terrified that someone will one day unmask you as a fraud. I understand. I have been where you are. This book, which you hold in your hands is the story of how God gently and so faithfully showed me how I didn't need that old mask anymore. How together with His help, we could destroy it. I don't need to hide behind it any longer. He wants to do that for you as well. My prayer for you today is this; that God will reveal to you the areas in your life where you are hiding behind a mask. That you will allow the gentleness of the Holy Spirit to begin to break the mask in pieces as you discover who you really are in Christ, and that when you walk in His freedom you no longer need to hide.

The Breakthrough

I would like to tell you that once I went to work I was all better. I'm sorry. That's just not the case. I went to work, and I did learn new skills; for example, how to keep that mask on very tightly and how to pretend all was well. I had too much work to do to think about anything else. I began to work ridiculous hours and began to acquire more responsibility quickly which lead to more hours. It is a vicious cycle that I fear too many people understand. My husband and I basically cohabitated because we were both working so much. It was during this time we began working toward our own home as most young marrieds do. With the good jobs we both had and the hours we worked it did not take as long as we thought to build up our credit and within the year we were looking at the possibility.

Would it surprise you to hear that our first house together was in fact the same house we attended home group in? It is a rather fun story how the Lord worked it out. It was a blessing to both couples. And soon we were moving into our own place. The transition to our own house went smoother than I expected and honestly for a while we were happy again. It began to seem like we were doing better and moving on, at least from the outside. From the inside I was still a mess.

We didn't talk about it...Hannah's death... but I needed to. Only I didn't know how. I didn't have the confidence to even share my deepest feelings with my own husband. I know now that it basically boiled down to trust. I did not trust anyone with knowing all of me. Now did my husband know more about me than anyone? Sure, he did! I told him almost everything. *Almost,* everything. He knew facts and dates and events, but he was never really given access to how I felt about those things. Or at least he wasn't given access until after stuffing so many things down and away that I would reach a limit and explode.

Do you know anyone like that? Perhaps you are like that. I would take my feelings, bottle them up so tight, stuff them into a can, until sometimes something so small would set it off like an atomic bomb. The poor guy didn't know what hit him. Why would it matter so much that we do not have eggs in the house? Seriously something so trivial could cause the top to go flying and a huge over reaction of emotion would come exploding out and then I would leave. Leave the room, leave the house or on one occasion leave the state! Many of these "blow-up" moments were triggered more from my fear of having failed. I failed to notice there were no eggs and therefore failed to do the shopping which meant I had failed to provide a decent meal for my husband which in turn reinforced the fact I was indeed a failure as a wife. Sound ridiculous? Sure, it does… Now. But my guess is there are some of you reading this that can actually relate. You feel like I may have a hidden camera into your house and could be telling your story. I promise you I don't. But God does. It is for you that this book had to be written. It is so that by reading and witnessing my story, that your story can be different too.

As I sit and type this part of the story my husband is reading a book in our bed. I sit and watch him and wonder what he will think when he holds this book in his hands. Will some of our earlier years be explained better to him or will he shake his head and say, "I don't remember that." *In truth, I hope he says the latter.* God has taught us both so much in twenty years. It is so much better now that God has healed my heart and soul that it is almost like writing about someone else. It can and will be like that for you as well. I promise you God will show up for you. He never disappoints those who are seeking for Him.

It was during the time we were getting ready to move into our house. I can't really tell you if it was over eggs or something else, but I can tell you exactly where I was standing when it happened. We were in the living room of our apartment near the hallway, surrounded by boxes, when he figured out all was not well, and all was not right. He had done something to upset me and all I did was purse my lips together and turn to walk away. See, I told you I was great at the running away from things. Or rather avoiding them. Either way, I was turning to leave the room. I will never forget the next few moments as long as I live. He grabbed my hand and pulled, turning me around. Then he lifted my head with his hand on my chin and jiggling my chin as you would a puppet he said these words, "I can't read your mind, you have to use your mouth, talk to me."

That was it, the dam broke, tears flooded to my eyes and spilled over my cheeks running down his hand and I said one of the most truthful and most difficult things to him I had ever said.

"I don't know how."

It may have been only a moment or minutes but as we stood there I finally voiced my true fear, "I am afraid of saying something wrong. That I will make you angry and that you will leave me."

It was then that he gave me a startling revelation... "You probably **will** say something that might make me angry. I obviously have said something to make you angry, but if you don't tell me what it is how will I know? How will we ever be able to make each other happy if we don't know what we are doing wrong to each other? I promised to stay during our wedding vows, remember? Just because we make each other mad doesn't mean we leave right? Are you leaving? Because, I'm not leaving."

I was so shocked that he thought I might be leaving him that the tears instantly stopped, and I looked at him in utter disbelief. "No."

"No... what?"

"No, I'm not leaving."

"Good, that's a start. Now what's wrong?"

And then we had a really real, heart to heart, no masks on, sort of awkward at times conversation. It is here that, nearly a year after her death I explained that I had a need to talk about our daughter. About how I missed her, and I wondered what she would be like now. How when he told me months ago men don't talk about this stuff, they go somewhere in their mind dig a deep hole put it there, bury it, and mark it with a small flag. So, when they want to go there and remember they can, but they don't talk about it; that I wasn't like that. But when he said it, it made me afraid to talk to him, that I was afraid of upsetting him. That I was hurting still, and I was sorry I had failed him by not keeping our child safe. That I had even failed at the very core thing that set me apart as female, bearing a child. I couldn't even do that right.

He held me as I cried for a long while. When the deluge of tears had ended we agreed to work harder on our communicating. Even as the words came tumbling out there was a fear in me that I would say too much or say it wrong and he would forever walk out the door because he would realize that he could find someone better than me. Someone who was not such a failure. He assured me I was not a failure, but that I was indeed the one he wanted to grow old with. We even cracked open the door of the conversation about adoption again.

Children of Healing

The Renewal

Having a download of emotion did alleviate that bottled up, pent up, stress and I was able to be happy about the new house and begin again to think about the possibility of filling that extra bedroom with another child. It had been over a year and we had agreed to birth control for three months, as the doctor suggested three to six months, but again due to side effects we did only the minimum of only three months. We knew we did want a family, and after all we now knew I could get pregnant! Phooey on the doctor from New York, what did she know! This time though, it would not be the same as it was the last time.

Because we both were working now, I had good health care coverage which required me to find another doctor. I spent quite a bit of time in prayer and doing research before I settled on a doctor. I ended up calling for a new patient appointment. It was about that time that I began to realize I had been working some crazy stupid hours and had a very high stress level. I was working sixty to eighty-hour work weeks. It began to take a toll on my body and we both knew that was not good. I mean I already knew my body seemed to have a mind of its own. In fact, I used to say that my body just hated me. I have since quit speaking those kinds of words over myself, even repenting for them, but at that time I really did believe it.

My first appointment was very difficult. Not only because those kind of doctor visits are uncomfortable anyway; but, then on top of that sharing the details of what I knew about my pregnancy with Hannah and her birth were still very tender. Dr. W was incredibly patient and very understanding and made me feel as if during that time I was the only one he needed to see that day. His nurse Liz was wonderful even holding my hand at one point because I had almost unconsciously reached for hers during my exam. We sat and figured out the time frame since Hannah's birth. It had been a year and a half, and we had not gotten pregnant while not taking any precautions, so the doctor wanted to start very conservatively. The first month he wanted me to cut down on my stress level, as well as wanting to give me medication that would cause my body to do what it should and then the next month we could talk about possible fertility options. After that he said something to me no doctor had ever said before. He asked me what I thought. Then, he sat there and actually waited for me to respond! I remember asking him, "What do you think I should do?" and he replied with, "No, this is your body not mine. It will be your decision, not mine."

I could hardly believe that he was saying something like that. I agreed with the conservative plan so during the first month I would focus on my health and he would look for my medical records and see if he could gain more information regarding my pregnancy with Hannah. He was very careful to not promise me anything to raise our hopes, but he also did not predict gloom and doom. I left there encouraged.

I had very much been considering taking some time off from work but didn't know how it would work. There were things I wanted to get done around the new house that would require my being there and working the crazy hours I did was not going to allow that. Plus, as we began to actively pursue the idea of trying to have another baby I had such a mix of emotions that I felt like a mess. I was so afraid of falling apart, which to my mind would have been a failure. So, I tried the whole using my mouth thing again and initiated a conversation with John. After, talking it over with him, I went to see the HR person at my work. I requested a personal leave of absence form. I ended up asking for the entire month of April off, without pay of course, for personal reasons. There was much speculation that I was actually going to quit, that I was leaving my husband, that I was having a secret health crisis, all kinds of crazy rumors. I assured many of my staff that none of these stories were true, that I just needed to get some stuff done.

I spent much of that month outside working in the yard. We leveled the front yard with truckloads and truckloads of dirt. Building the stone retaining wall was very challenging but spending so much time alone outdoors gave me time to think and pray. And then more time to pray and think. I began to realize my anger was dissipating but the aching in my heart was still so raw. It was during this month off that I attended my first ever women's retreat. Many women from our church were going over to beautiful Cannon Beach, Oregon. My mom and I decided to go. It truly was a life changing weekend for me.

Before I tell you about what God did at the retreat I think you should know something. I think it will resonate with someone. It is important for you to know that I did talk about Hannah with people. I would share with them about our daughter who was in heaven. How I knew beyond all doubt that she was with the Father and that she was a part of my future. I would allow women to share their secret grief over miscarriages that they were never allowed to talk about. I am still amazed at the number of women who seem genuinely pleased and shocked when I ask them their child's name. Many of them never spoke the name they had chosen, to anyone, until they told it to me. Some had not even told their spouse. I hold these memories and precious names in a special place in my heart.

I have had the opportunity to share with and allow, so many women the ability to freely grieve for their children and look to the future with the hope of seeing them again. I hug them and pray with them and encourage them. I reassure them that their husbands do care, but that men really do grieve differently than we women do. I have shared what my husband said to me. I can see shimmers of hope return to places in their souls as we share about our children and our hope of seeing them again.

At the retreat I was able to talk with one lady in the hallway. Why I remember her so much I think is because as I listened to her tell me the story of the baby she lost and then was never allowed to talk about, I could see and feel all the raw pain and anger built up inside her. I asked her what her baby's name was. She said we didn't name her really, but I always knew she was a girl and that I would call her Tess. I assured her Tess was a lovely name and that I was sure now that we had met, Hannah and Tess would most likely meet, and wait for us together. Her eyes told me a story I knew all too well. I began to tell her that God wanted to take all that from her. It was not His desire for her to walk around defeated and broken inside. As the words tumbled out I knew I was talking to myself as well as to her.

When our conversation had ended I needed to take a long walk on the beach alone with my thoughts and the Lord. As I walked barefoot along the beach just praying, remembering, and thinking, I began to see a purpose rising from my pain. In a moment of honesty, removing my mask with another, we both had a moment with God the Healer of our souls. It was that day the seeds of this book were first sowed.

On the last day of the retreat there was an optional worship service in which you could participate. Most all the women showed up because by then God had already ministered in some amazing ways. It was here in the midst of worship, God touched my heart. As the worship filled the room some women knelt down at the front altar area, others danced in the back. I found myself near a wall divider in quite a private little area. I began to worship, and the tears began to flow, and I began to recall the conversation with Tess's mom. I found I could not control the weeping and I ended up with my face on the floor sobbing uncontrollably as that day in the hallway of the apartment. I felt all the emptiness, all the aching as if my chest and heart were hollow.

As I lay there I felt the Lord say to me, "One more time," and I knew what He meant. I knew that this would be the last time I ever mourned that deeply again. I poured out all my heart to Him. All my tears. All my grief. He began to close the raw gaping wound. When I finally stood up from that floor, nearly an hour later, the deep, ever - present throbbing ache in my chest was no longer there. I knew I would always miss her and think about her and wonder. But that deep unfathomable aching would no longer haunt me. I also knew when I stood up there would be another child and that this child would not be a replacement, but its own placement. There was a family for me and not this next child or any after it would ever take the place of my first child. It was not until then I realized I had not been ready to have another child. I had needed the healing hand of God to move in me and restore me before I could ever have another baby. God is so good and faithful, knowing

• • •
76

what we need instead of just giving us what we think we want. I think also that weekend a bit of the mask was removed. I had revealed a true part of me and found value and worth.

Children of Healing

The Promise

When I returned to work the first of May, I returned differently than when I left. I made up my mind that there were things that could wait, and I began to give some priorities to my own health and family. I had not returned very long, when it seemed I would need to change areas and relinquish some status if I was going to keep my newly found priorities. So, I did. I composed a letter to the Director of Nurses and offered to switch floors to a position I knew they needed to fill. This meant stepping down from a management position that I was in. Or, if she did not see that as a good trade, then she could consider this my thirty days' notice.

She was indeed shocked and yet did not want me to leave and so at the end of the month I stepped down. Instantly my stress level dropped. I was no longer required at multiple daily and weekly meetings. State paperwork for funding was no longer my responsibility; and, at the end of my shift, I could go home. I will say though, that because I was fully aware of those responsibilities I was a very good charge nurse; trying my best, while on duty, to help out the manager of the floor I had transferred to. If you know someone else's job, along with the stress they are under, the requirements they need to meet, and it is in your ability to help; alleviate some of that stress by not just doing your job but doing it well, maybe take that one little extra step. You will find people will always want you on their team. It is a lesson taught to us in the New Testament about going the extra mile.

It would be lie if I told you I did not have a few thoughts of failure by stepping down from my position. But then this time was different because it was a conscious choice. I was realigning my priorities. I was beginning to trust God more, because I knew God was going to bless us with a family. That I would, in His timing, have the job I desired most - motherhood. If you find yourself in a season of change and you feel as if God has you moving backward instead of forward, take heart. Sometimes in a season of transition we can feel as if we have failed. Although, it may be highly likely that there is a plan and a growth process that needs to occur because God is preparing you for the next thing.

It is at times like this we need to remind ourselves that waiting is actually a verb. It is an action word. When you are waiting you are doing something. You must participate in the waiting process, it is the growing season. A farmer cannot harvest a crop he planted only a day ago. The seeds must be tended and waited upon as they grow. The farmer will water, fertilize, aerate, and pull weeds. All in the hope of giving his seed the best chance at producing an abundant harvest. Our times of waiting are much like this. We water and fertilize by reading and studying God's Word. We aerate the ground and pull weeds by guarding our hearts and purging that which is not of Him. Worship Him in times of waiting and you will find your harvest will be abundant in His time. However, if you waste your time of waiting, you will reap the harvest that you have tended; full of weeds and little fruit.

When I returned to the doctor he was again gentle and straightforward. He gave all the options for fertility treatments, starting very conservatively and going up from there. The decision would be mine. He offered me no false hope. He clearly stated he could not promise that nothing would go wrong, but he said, "From all the tests I have run and what I have read in your history nothing leads me to believe that it definitely will happen again. I have every belief that you will get pregnant and carry to full term." Now that my heart had been touched and restored I had every hope and belief for that as well, so we proceeded with the lowest possible fertility medication first.

Again, I would love to tell you it was that easy. That once was all it took but it wasn't. It was four months later before we were pregnant. We all rejoiced and cried when he confirmed the pregnancy. The doctor monitored me very closely during the next several months. Probably more for my own state of mind and reassurance than for his, but it was marvelous to go into the office and hear that little fast paced heartbeat. I would cry every time and every time I would thank God for His promise. We had several ultrasounds to monitor the amniotic fluid levels because they were lower than normal levels. At one point he gave me strict orders to be drinking three quarts of water a day, to help maintain hydration for both of us. I became very attached to my water cup and the bathroom!

When I think back on it now, I believe God's hand was even in this. For the thing this could have caused me to panic. What it allowed was extra appointments so there would be a constant reassurance for us that the baby really was growing fine and doing well. It was not until we passed the twenty-week mark that I sort of relaxed. You would think that with as many checkups and ultrasounds that we had we would have found out the sex of the baby fairly early. In truth the little stinker would never move in such a way that we could tell, though it was not for lack of trying on the part of the technician. It was our last ultrasound before the baby was due that we found out we were having a girl. We would call her Katie.

Up until then I really did not care what the baby would be as long as the baby was healthy. It was in the quiet moments alone back at home that I began to understand that I had been afraid of another girl. Afraid of a repeat, even though I knew God had it under control. I believe there had been a part of me still untrusting. That night as I lay awake with my thoughts and prayers to God, I thanked Him that we had reached this point not knowing, because now we had reached a point that should I go into labor the baby would survive.

There are times in our lives where we think that we want to know. Times when we wish God would just tell us the plan. Tell us the details because we think we need to know. Although, the truth really can be that if we knew everything, we would be frightened. Sometimes He withholds details until we are really, really ready for them. Can you trust today that perhaps, the answer you seek for has not been revealed to you yet because the Author of the plan knows that you are not ready for the information? He knows us better than we do ourselves. We are really good at deceiving ourselves and God can see past all that. If I leave you with any one bit of information about God, let it be this... God is Trustworthy. Trust Him my friends. He is who He says He is and He will do what He says He will do.

On the 24th of March I woke up like every day wondering if today was "the" day. I was finding the wait to be hard because I no longer had work to occupy my time. The doctor had taken me off work early because my blood pressure had started climbing, not uncommon in late pregnancy but we were taking all precautions. As it turned out I began leaking fluid, but I was not having any contractions. John had to go into work so as he was getting ready I called the doctor's office. He said to go into the hospital just to check and see if I was leaking amniotic fluid but because there was no sign of labor, yet it probably was nothing. Because we expected nothing John continued onto work with instructions to page him a 9-1-1 page if I was being admitted at the hospital. (For the younger crowd reading this you have to understand this was a time before everyone had a cell phone.) My husband carried a pager for work and I never had used a 9-1-1 page with him before, so this was going to be a signal for him. If it was nothing, I would page him with the house number when I returned home.

My mom drove me to the hospital. The nurse checked the leaking fluid and then announced, "Congratulations, you are going to be our guest for the night." I was indeed leaking amniotic fluid but what they thought was happening is that it was only a tear and not as though my water had broken, so my body had not gotten the message to start contractions. We paged John 9-1-1, and almost immediately he was at the hospital. I accused him of speeding terribly. Then he explained when he received the page he was already in the hospital parking lot! Since the hospital was on his way home and he had not heard from me he decided to check there before going on home. He was circling the lot looking for Mom's car when I paged him.

I was hooked up to many monitors and medicine to induce my labor was started. Then we waited, and we waited, and we waited. I would have liked to get up and walk around but I was not allowed to. It was not long into the labor that the low levels of amniotic fluid were an issue and they had to start adding fluid back for the baby as she was compressing the umbilical cord which was causing her stress and she would set off the heart monitor. She began having heart decelerations. It was a long, long night. I had wires and cords hooked to me everywhere; some were for me, some were for her.

The next morning the doctor came in and sat down in a chair right by my head. I knew in that moment what he was coming to say. I had hoped it would not come to that and he knew it. He stated the facts about how long it had been since I started leaking, how my blood pressure was climbing, how my body wasn't reacting well to the medicine and how the baby's heartbeat kept fluctuating. Then he said, "What is our goal?" We both knew what the goal was: a happy, healthy baby. Before I could answer, the alarm for the baby's heart monitor was going off again. *The baby was in trouble!* His face said as much to me as I am sure mine did to him. "It's time, isn't it?" was all I could say. He nodded his head and I did mine. It was agreed. The doctor was up, out the door, and giving orders. The nurses snapped into action and were already starting to wheel my bed out the door and to the operating room.

I was shocked to see it had already been prepared and there were people waiting on us. As the doctor began scrubbing in, another nurse took John somewhere to change as I was rapidly being prepped by two more nurses. Once in the operating room, things happened so quickly. I believe the doctor even started before John got his scrubs on. When John returned he was accompanied by my mom, also dressed in scrubs. It was only a matter of minutes before we heard that little cry! The tears would not stop running down my face. I had not even seen her yet but the very sound of her voice moved me to tears of thankfulness that even now spill over my cheeks at the thought of it. It was the sound I had longed to hear two and a half years earlier - but did not. When the doctor showed her to me my eyes were so full of tears I couldn't see. The anesthesiologist wiped my eyes, so I could see her clearly.

She was whisked away and immediately handed off to a waiting nurse and stand-by doctor. I quickly looked to John begging him to stay with her assuring him I was ok. He quickly went to her side. I was so overwhelmed I began to cry and shake; it was such a relief to hear her, to hear the nurse calling out her vitals and to have my doctor step up by my face and say, "She's here, she's beautiful, she's alive." I know there was a strange look given to him from the other nurse and doctor in the room, but it did not matter. All I could say over and over was, "Thank you, thank you, thank you," as the tears ran freely and heavily. My thanks were to not only to the doctor but to God as well. I do believe the doctor knew that. He smiled and then said, "Now, let's get this finished up and be done here."

I could go into so much detail here and tell you all that happened in the next moments and days that followed but I am willing to bet you don't need me to do that. After reading this book this far you will surely understand the sheer JOY that filled my heart and soul. Like all new moms there was much learning to do. The first several nights I am not sure if there was any sleeping at all, especially the first night home alone. No nurses, no doctor, just us. I watched her while she slept just to see her breathe. I will admit to putting my hand under her nose or jiggling her from time to time when she was so still that I couldn't tell if she was breathing.

It was wonderful being home with her. I was happier than I could recall in such a long time. God had done what He said. He had given us another child and, in my eyes, she was perfect. However, the cardiologist had something else to say about that. Even before we left the hospital we had a visit from the pediatrician. They had detected a heart murmur. We were scheduled for an appointment before we even left the hospital. I suppose you would think that I panicked; and given my history you would think so, but God gave me this overwhelming peace. As I snuggled my infant daughter who was alive and breathing in my arms I knew God had given her to us and I was not frightened. It would be completely untruthful if I said we didn't pray about it, or seek the prayers of others, but I was never concerned for her life. I had a promise from God and I stood on it.

There is much I could tell you about how God has moved and how He has been shown mighty when it comes to the dealings of Katie's heart; however, that is for another time and even for another storyteller – Her. It is her testimony of God's healing power and I love to hear her tell it. But, before we leave that subject know this; God can perform surgery without doctors! Even while your children sleep. I can prove it to you with scripture. He did surgery on Adam while he slept and created Eve. He healed the dead girl who lay as though she were sleeping. These things God did instantly, but

He can also heal over time when you have no idea its happening, then suddenly one day the outcome is made known. Continue to pray, continue to seek, and continue to stand on the promise He has given to you!

The first appointment with my doctor after the birth was a happy one. I was recovering well from the C-section. He was pleased. As with all postpartum appointments there was the birth control talk. *Seriously? Was he kidding?* After all we had been through to get to this point, all the work it took to get pregnant, did he really think I was worried about birth control? But in his wisdom, he cautioned me, insuring me, now that my body had been through the process it might just have figured it out. All I could think was *YEAH RIGHT!!* I went home and chuckled most the way there. You know, I didn't think about it until just this moment, but there was another woman in the Bible who laughed at the thought of having a child. Sarah believed it to be impossible for her to have a child also because of her history. God would prove her wrong. You can read all about it in Genesis chapter eighteen. God would also laugh and prove me wrong.

It was the 4th of July. We had plans with my parents but first we would get to sleep in if the baby would let us. I coaxed her back to sleep with a bottle and was thankful for a few extra minutes when suddenly I felt an overwhelming urge to vomit. As I rushed to the bathroom I had begun an immediate argument in my head. I couldn't be sick, it was a holiday, we had plans. Maybe I wasn't sick. Maybe it was food poisoning. What did I eat, was it uncooked chicken or something? Go ahead… again… feel free to laugh with me. I am absolutely one hundred percent sure that the question, *"Do you think you could possibly be pregnant?"* was not my own thought. As a matter of fact, thinking back on it, I bet the Lord even said it with a hint of a chuckle. I know it was not my thought because it stopped me cold. Standing in the bathroom I slowly turned toward the mirror to look at myself and said, "Do you think?"

It was only a fraction of a second before I was digging out from under the sink a pack of pregnancy tests that was still left behind from the months previous. There was still a test in there. I took it. Yes indeed. Two pink lines appeared right there while I was still holding it, I didn't even have to wait the allotted three minutes.

It's quite funny to hear my husband tell the next part of the story. As he tells it, I jumped on the bed waking him up and waving a still dripping test in his face. I don't recall it going quite like that at all. I recall being shocked and immediately elated and yet concerned about what others might say. I did wake him up but I waited for him to sleep in… a little.

When my parents arrived to commence the holiday plans, I left them briefly in the office with John and walked to the bathroom, feeling a bit queasy again. It was from there I could hear him say, "So… Did Karrie tell you?" *What?! Was he really…* I began running to the office, *what was he thinking? I hadn't confirmed anything. Was he seriously telling them?* I heard the words "She's Pregnant!" As I rushed into the room. He is smiling a

89

great big huge toothy grin. Dad and Mom look at him, then me, then him again. For added emphasis he adds, "She took a test this morning." They all turn and look at me again. I feel my face flush red hot. Mom starts laughing as Dad jumps up from the futon clapping his hands together shouting, "Well ALRIGHT, Joshua is on his way!" Joshua was the name we had had picked for a boy since we had been pregnant with Hannah. Next thing I know, Dad is hugging me, bouncing around, nearly dancing with Joy. I am still stunned. Stunned and nauseous. My concerns over what people might think, definitely did not apply to my parents.

There were many though, who felt it necessary to point out to us that our Katie was still a newborn herself, and didn't we know what caused that, and were we crazy, and other such things. But, besides my dad's reaction, the next best face was that of my doctor. Sitting in his office for a follow up after the C-section, an appointment I had already scheduled, I explained to him I thought I was pregnant again. His face broke into a huge grin, like your granddad would do when something happened just the way he explained it would and it still surprised you anyway. Yeah, it was that kind of look. I believe my exact next words were, "Let's just say I didn't believe you and leave it at that." He chuckled then said, "okay." And we did.

This pregnancy would be a much more relaxed one and yet busy because I was still dealing with an infant at home. But the fear that seemed to be my constant companion during the pregnancy with Katie did not plague me with this one. It did indeed turn out to be Joshua. Because there was only two months of non-pregnant time between the pregnancies, at the end of this one, I felt as if I had been pregnant for forever. He was quite a bit bigger and I was much more uncomfortable near the end. The day it was time to go to the hospital we knew it would be another C-section. I felt a bit more prepared this time.

One of the best things about his birth I will never forget was the fact I knew he was born before the doctor said so, because for the first time in months I could actually take a deep breath. The doctor shouted, "He's here!" And with my first deep breath I said, "I know!" It was then he started to cry and instantly my new-found breath caught in my throat. His cry sounded different, it was a new different voice. It was as if in that moment in time a huge reality that should have already occurred to me, broke through barrier of my mind. This was a whole new and different child. Of course, his voice would sound different from his sister, but honestly until I heard him, it never occurred to me. It was then my own tears began to run down my face. God had given me a gift, an unexpected little boy who, from that first cry, stole a piece of my heart.

Children of Healing

The Blessing

After years of hardship and heartache thinking I would never get to experience motherhood, I suddenly found myself in it. Two times over in less than a year. It truly is the hardest and most satisfying job in the world. I very much enjoyed being a nurse but taking care of and raising my own babies was even better. I could so easily go into story after story of cuteness with my children. I loved watching the wonder in their eyes as they witnessed new things daily. The trips to the zoo. The first sucker. The newness of spring after the first winter of snow and snowmen. In truth it is through these moments the Lord began to reveal to me more love than I ever imagined. He began to show me more of His character and just how He saw me. All the love I had in my heart for my babies He had for me.

Perhaps you too, at times, have questioned the love the Father has for you. I pray that even as you read this book that God begins to show you more of His great Love, that you begin to see yourself through His eyes. Not just the way you think He sees you, but how He really does. This was a prayer that I prayed almost daily, during those years, as I sought to know Him more. *Lord, show me how you see me. Not how I see myself but how YOU really do.* This amazing God must love me; because He took the time, to care about me, to bless me with my greatest desire, a family of my own. I began to really seek Him. To read about Him. And had a deep desire for more of Him.

The flip side of really seeking Him, really wanting to know Him more is becoming more aware of who you are. As you press into Him, be prepared for Him to press into you. He will begin to show you and reveal to you, areas that He desires to see you change or places He desires to heal. Those areas He wants for you to hand over or abandon for your own good. This can be a beautiful process. And also, a difficult one.

Sometimes when the Lord desires to teach us things the process can be very lengthy. It seems we think we figured it out and then there is another lesson or another layer so to speak. I have often heard the analogy that it is like peeling the layers of an onion. When we peel away one layer there is another one underneath. Some people describe it as going deeper. And still others consider it as climbing to a higher level, going from glory to glory. Whichever one of these works for you, the point is the same; learning with God is a process. It is a bit easier to talk about the process now several years afterward rather than when in the midst of it. But the fact remains - the process took longer than for you to read this book! Why do I say that to you? For this one main reason: Do not become frustrated with the process. Embrace it. Encourage it. For the real secret to walking out this life is, it really is about the journey, not just the destination.

If you have ever taken a long road trip with your family, then you can understand. It is the long hours of conversation, sometimes deep, sometimes silly, sometimes reminiscent, and the crazy "side of the road" pit stops with the creepy stuffed mammals or the moments of "sure, let's eat junk food instead of a real dinner" that turn a road trip into a memorable family vacation. Even the wrong turns or the missed roads become a part of the story. Years later it is those seemingly insignificant parts of the trip that make the smiles appear when all that was said is, "Remember when we took a trip to such and such..." Where ever the trip ended it is the telling of getting there and getting back and the process that make the stories great. Our learning patterns and growth process with God are really no different. I mean, aren't those some of the best parts of the stories in the Bible too? What would the story of the Exodus be if we didn't get the ten plagues beforehand? Or if we are just told the Israelites got out of Egypt but left out the part about walking through the Red Sea while escaping. Consider the story of Joseph saving Egypt during the famine, while leaving out how he first got there because he was thrown in a pit and sold as a slave. Or leaving out the whole, falsely accused and thrown in prison, part?

My point here is simple; don't get off track because you are frustrated with the length of your journey or the time spent in a rest area. All of these add up to your process, your journey. I very firmly believe we will all enjoy movie night in heaven as we watch the story of you or the story of me. I trust that even the things I still do not understand will be made absolutely clear to me there. That we will see what God was doing and working out for us as we were sitting on the side of the road with a flat tire or laid up in that bed for months.

We need to remind ourselves continually that God is trustworthy, and He has a plan. If I am seeking God's guidance and staying humble before Him, I will reach the end of the journey and I just might help out a few others along the way.

It was a few years after our son was born that the Lord led us down another road we hadn't necessarily planned to take. We adopted our youngest child after relocating from Washington to Texas. The idea of adopting had been discussed not long after our doctor visit that started this whole book, and again after Hannah died. However, it resurfaced several times and again after our daughter started kindergarten.

Our son was lonely and came to me one day very matter of factly and declared that he NEEDED a brother. To be perfectly honest the initial reaction I had in my head was one of laughter, (remember how that went for me before) but the words that came out my mouth were not laughing at all. I looked at my son and with all seriousness said, "Well then, you had better pray about that then." I think I was the one more shocked by the response than he was. All he did was shake his little head in agreement and walk away. I began to talk to the Lord, wondering why I had said what I did. I reasoned it away; explaining to him that Momma couldn't have any more babies would either be too complicated for him to understand or it would deflate the cute little face staring up at me. In fact, the whole thing struck me funny. I immediately shared the encounter with my husband and then my parents.

I will tell you that little boy did not take it as a funny little conversation. He began to pray faithfully every night, unprompted, for a brother. During the day he began to pretend that he had five brothers, each one had a special talent that he was good at. It went on like this for a while and I began to feel as though this was more than just a passing phase. This started me taking it before the Lord as well. Knowing full well that a baby was not coming from my womb, the Lord began to show me that one could come to us from somewhere else. Hadn't we already had an adoption conversation many years ago when we thought we couldn't have our own? I began to pray if we were to adopt another child that God would tell John, because I wasn't going to. I also knew if God was indeed bringing another child to us, I needed even then to begin to pray for him. You see, if Joshua was so sure it was a boy then I figured it was going to be a boy and that I should keep him in prayer too. Even then I seemed to know He would not be a baby. But again, God would have to tell John. So, I waited and prayed. Several months went by and then through a very "only God could do this," series of events we were on our way to becoming foster parents with a fast track to adoptive parents.

I say fast track, but the truth is, it was just a week or so shy of nine months from the time our son first entered our home until the court officially declared him a Manning. I think one of my most precious memories during those first few days was coming around the hallway corner and seeing my two boys sitting on the top step. It was as if an invisible hand stopped me in my tracks, because I was heading down those stairs, but I was halted and allowed to observe.

The boys were five and half and just barely four. They were sitting side by side on the top step of the stairs. I have no idea how long they had been there or why on Earth they would even think to just sit down right there and have a conversation, but that is what they were doing, sitting and talking. The oldest brother had his arm across the shoulders of the younger. Holding him close and looking very intently into his younger brother's face the oldest said, "You know, I am so glad you are here. You know, I prayed for you." I immediately turned around so as not to interrupt this private moment and rushed to the side of my bed. I was on my knees crying in half a second. I have no doubt in my mind that we certainly do have little brother because of the fervent insistent prayer of a little boy who just knew God would bring him a brother if only he asked.

The process of the adoption as I said took nine months. The day I figured that out, I told the Lord half laughing, "Well, that was the hardest pregnancy and labor yet Father!" You know those moments of the road trip when you feel like you took a wrong turn. And then you end up miles from where you thought you should be, but while you are there you see some of the most amazing sights of the whole journey. It was a bit like that. I mean God definitely had His hand in it the whole way even if we didn't see how or why things would turn out like they did. When God takes you on a road trip He tends to operate on a need to know basis. Most of the time I guess He figures we don't need to know! Our human mind will tell us that we need an answer as to why, or how, or when. But, the true reality of trusting God is doing it by faith. Only by faith. There will be times when your faith will take you places others will not understand. As is true with Abraham in the Old Testament. I am sure many family members balked as he packed up everything to go somewhere no one knew, not even him. The same was true for some of our family; they did not understand the move to Texas. But we knew we needed to go and as a result, we became the family of five we are today.

If you know God has called you to do something, may I encourage you to step out in faith and do it. It may not make sense to those around you. It may, in fact, seem crazy to them. But if you are sure God called you to do it, then, DO IT! Some of God's biggest rewards in my life were from stepping out terrified but in obedience to Him. You hold in your hands now one of those things for me. It is solely an act of obedience that has me writing this book right now. But I have learned enough over the years to understand He will have a purpose for it and I eagerly await His timing to see what He does with it.

I have learned that God will do things for a couple different reasons, to grow or mature me. This seems pretty self-explanatory; however, we will return to this subject. Or to grow or mature someone using me. This is very humbling and to this day still amazes me. Now back to maturing me, sometimes this is a nice simple thing like attend this conference and come away with a nice little nugget of truth all wrapped up pretty like. But sometimes God continues out a plan that I do not yet know all the details of or even the end result but will eventually be informed of. This one can be difficult because it requires blind faith. During our adoption process there were a lot of moments of just having faith and nothing else. Faith that God had a plan, even if we had no idea what it might be. There were some very difficult moments that the Lord walked us through. Partly because our son was not an infant.

If you have ever been or known a foster parent or adoptive parent, then you are already aware that there is much about a child that is only discovered once they are in your home. Truthfully, any parent can say this same thing, even bringing home their infant from the hospital.

We spend so much time learning our babies only to discover they changed what they liked overnight. Isn't that the truth when it comes to feeding a toddler? One minute they have to have chicken nuggets: and the next, it's cheerios; and only cheerios will do. Imagine if you will, a toddler whom you have never met before. Where do you even begin to start?

Much of our early days were very much like this. Not only were we learning a new person, but we were also learning a whole new, damaged person. We not only had to figure out likes and dislikes we had to learn triggers and timing and how to defuse a little ticking time bomb before it exploded. I suppose some reading this will feel that analogy to be an overreaction, but I assure you it isn't. Much of my son's first three years are not the kind of story that makes for happy endings. I am quite thankful he has hardly any memory of these times in his life. It is only because of God that he is the person he is today.

I tell you these things because we are talking about life journeys. Our journey, through this life, here on planet Earth. There will be a day when we will not have to endure the hardships of this physical place any longer. But until then, I believe we are here to learn and to help each other. By sharing my story, my prayer is that you are encouraged, uplifted, and strengthened to continue your journey, your process. Sometimes the stories are happy and silly; sometimes they are serious and sad. No matter what they are they also intertwine.

One day very vividly I knew the Lord had spoken to me. I was struggling with some behaviors with our son that seemed insurmountable. I was frustrated and angry. I'm sure none of you have ever felt that way with your kids... Yes, that was sarcasm. I know every parent has days like that. It was one of those days. I sat on the couch and watched the tantrum unfolding before me and very clearly heard in my spirit. "You cannot help him deal with his junk, if you don't let me deal with yours."

Can I just tell you, the truth of that statement hit me hard! Let's get real for a moment. I doubt there is a person on this planet old enough to read this book that doesn't have "stuff." We all have "stuff." Some people just carry it around and manage it better than others. Can I tell you today, God doesn't want you to have to "manage" anything! He sent Jesus to earth to carry all that for you. Jesus died with all that on himself, so you would not have to bear the weight of it. And Jesus rose from the dead so that you could walk in the hope and victory of not carrying that kind of luggage.

It doesn't matter what your "stuff" is. It could be stuff you did or didn't do. It could be stuff done to you or not done for you. It can be physical stuff or mental stuff. It can be future stuff or present stuff or past stuff. We all have stuff. Whether it's known to others or only known to you and God. I may not be the first one to tell you this, but there is nothing too big for God. It's True! Remember how we talked about Him being big enough to handle all the things you feel? He is also big enough to handle all the "stuffs" that you have.

No one on this planet is perfect. Not you and certainly not me! Not your parents. Not your children. Not your boss. Not even the pastor of your local church. You may have heard a familiar Bible verse that says, *"For all have sinned and fall short of the Glory of God. Romans 3:23."* Notice the key word in there is… ALL. Not just some. ALL. I am an ALL and you are an ALL. God came so that you don't have to live in a place of defeat.

Walking through nightmares and speech struggles and learning struggles with our son, I began to have more compassion, more patience, more love. As my heart ached to give him the better life we felt he deserved God began to deal with my heart about the life He thought I deserved. Did you know God has thoughts like that? He told us that He did. It says in John 10:10 *"I have come that you might have life, and that you might have it more abundantly."*

Think about that a minute. Life that is more abundant than the one you have right now. What does that look like to you? More money? More peace? More security? Less fear? Less worry? Less stress? I bet you have a list of your own. What if I said God had an even bigger list for you! Above what you could ever ask or imagine. Would you find it hard to believe? I did too, once.

This year our Hannah would have been eighteen. When I look back on the time that has passed it seems like an eternity and yet it seems like yesterday. Yesterday, because I can recall some of the details with extreme clarity and an eternity because I have learned so much since then. The one thing I pray you take away more than anything else after reading some of my story is this. God IS trustworthy.

He can be trusted when all is well. He can be trusted when the storm is raging around you so hard you feel every cell in your body is just fighting to keep your head above the rising water. God can be trusted. If no one else in your life can be trusted... God can be trusted. He is the one who will never let you down. Even if the circumstances are not what you would think ideal, He can be trusted. When your heart feels so crushed and shattered, even beaten beyond repair - God can be trusted to gently restore it. When your child is sick - God can be trusted. When your spouse leaves - God can be trusted. When addiction threatens to destroy all that you hold dear - God can be trusted. When your parents pass away. When you have been evicted. When sickness is eating your body. God can be trusted.

Do you find this hard to believe? In truth, so did I. I mean, I knew it in my intellect because I had been taught it from the time I was a little girl, actually before I was born. You see my momma read the Bible out loud to us before we were born. My twin brother and I always knew we were miracles. We knew God had healed my mother and we were the direct result of that healing. But can I tell you knowing it in your mind and knowing it in your heart of hearts right down to the marrow of your bones, is entirely different.

Learning to trust the Lord with this deep kind of conviction did not happen for me over night and I am sure it will be a process for you as well. My hope is that by reading this book, your trust factor in God levels up. That can, and does, happen when we see how God helped someone else, and provided for someone else, and proved Himself for someone else. This is why we have been given a rich history of God in the Bible. I understand though, it is nice to read about someone we can look at and touch. Someone we can point to and say, "Have you heard how God helped her?" I pray that I am that example in people's lives.

Be encouraged today my friends, God loves you. God cares about what you care about. God has a plan and a desire for you. A plan laid out just for you. God loves you so much. God did not just come to this planet because Karrie was going to fall apart when her daughter died. God did not come to this planet just because Karrie needed to know that no matter what her past, she is redeemable. God came because you were going to struggle. You were going to face addiction. You were going to have your heart broken and need a Savior. One who understood the need of healing not only the physical but also the internal. The secret hiding places of your heart. God is trustworthy because He is Love. He loves us so much. God. Can. Be. Trusted.

What do you need to hear Him say to you today? What do you need to say to Him today? Prayer is the fancy little word we use for just simply talking to God and letting Him talk to you. Friend, God desperately wants to talk with you. He longs to be with you. He longs to hold you in his arms like a new mom longs to hold her newborn child. When our middle son was born he had struggled to breathe and was rushed off to the nursery. I only saw his cute little face. It took them longer with me in the operating room than expected and by the time I was returned to a hospital room my son was four hours old and I had not yet been able to hold him. When the nurse came in to check on me I burst into tears and cried out, "Can't I please hold my baby?" After reading this book I am sure it is not a stretch for your imagination to know what kind of thoughts were flying through my mind, having already lost a baby. My arms ached to hold him. Friends, God aches to hold you the same way. He loves you so much and has great plans and desires for you and it pains His heart to see His children struggle knowing He has what they need and can comfort them.

But as I have already said to you, God is also a gentleman. He will never force Himself upon you. We were given free will. It is our choice to allow God into the middle of our situations. He wants so much to be there, but it is up to us to allow Him access. Someone needs to hear that again. God will not force His will upon you, Friend. Sometimes we stay in our pain because we refused to let God have it. I understand that. I have been there, done that. But, can I tell you, walking in His freedom and grace, because I let Him have those secret places, is so much better!

Ask Him. Invite God into the most secret, most tender places of your heart and He who is trustworthy, will heal you. God has used the process of all my children to heal the inner most parts of my soul and I know He can and will do the same for you. Allow Him to gently have that which you cling to so hard. You know, not only will God NOT force you to give Him your heart, He is also gentle enough to say I can help you to give that to me. It does not take some hugely eloquent prayer, that you have to recite so many times or while standing on your head on the third Tuesday under a crescent moon. Yes, that was meant to be a bit humorous, because so many times we over complicate what God intended to be so easy.

Use your words, as simple as you think they are. Be honest with Him. Tell Him what is going on inside you. The truth is God already knows but by engaging in a conversation with Him about it, you are allowing him access to it. God will meet you where you are. He does not dangle carrots for you to have to chase. Let Him lead you. Give your heart fully to Him. Find a home church where others will seed into your life and where you can also seed into others. You have a destiny. God does want to use you. Start seeking it out. Read His words to you. They have been written down for thousands of years and they are still relevant to us today.

Before you go I would like to pray over you.

*Father, I ask for you to reveal more of yourself to my
friends. That you Lord, would become so real to them that
they can feel your tangible presence with them even now.*
*Holy Spirit, you are the Spirit of Truth, bring truth
to them this day.*
*Remove confusion and bring clarity. May the Love of
God penetrate the deepest, darkest, most secret places of their
heart.*
*Lord, heal that which is broken. Mend the soul as
only you can.*
*May they give you entrance into those areas that they
have previously resisted.*
*Pursue each and every one of your children in such a
way that they know, you desire to be with them and talk to
them.*
Show them the plans you have for them.
*May they know today the Joy and the Freedom of
complete surrender unto You.*
*May the truth, that you are trustworthy, and that you
love them never leave them.*
*Long after they forget the words they have read here
may they remember the truths you taught them along the way.*
I Love you Lord.
I ask this in Jesus mighty name.
Amen

Dear Friends

When asking myself the reason for publishing this book, I really had to seek the Lord. I have shared this story or rather fragments of this story many times. Why take the time and effort to put it on paper? Certainly, I am convinced this book will end up places that I will never go and find its way to hands I will not have the privilege to shake. And why does it need to?

You, my friends are the answer. I know beyond doubt that my family is not the only family to have experienced a great loss. I also know that many who walk the dark road through such a loss sometimes stumble and lose their way. They can become numb and despondent. Some will even begin to question God. Some I will be given the great privilege of being able to hug in person, yet others I will only touch with my words.

I will not pretend to have all the answers, but my prayer is, as I have been very transparent in sharing how God healed my heart, that others will begin to heal as well. I pray they see that God truly is good and He absolutely can be trusted. It still astounds me how God continues to use the death and life of my children to teach me. God can be trusted with all the shattered pieces of our hearts and skillfully mold them into a whole and completed masterpiece.

Because He has done such a great work in me how can I remain silent? I cannot! He surely has called me, and I must declare the wonder and the greatness of my God.

The Word says in

Isaiah 61:1-3
The Spirit of the Lord God is upon me,
Because He has anointed me, to preach good tidings to the poor;
He has sent me to heal the brokenhearted,
To proclaim liberty to the captives,
And the opening of the prison to those who are bound; To
proclaim the acceptable year of the Lord,
And the day of vengeance of our God;
To comfort all who mourn,
To console those who mourn in Zion,
To give them beauty for ashes,
The oil of Joy for mourning,
The garment of praise for the spirit of heaviness;
That they may be called trees of righteousness,
The planting of the Lord, that He may be glorified.

The emphasis here is mine, but I really believe that this is the heart and soul behind the publishing of this book. A broken heart can only be fully mended when surrendered to our loving Savior Jesus Christ. He came to this Earth as a babe with nothing so that you might not lack. He walked among us teaching about the Father's love so that you might understand. He was beaten and crucified, taking the punishment for my sins and yours. And then He also arose from the dead to bring us the hope of a future.

My friends, my future holds great treasure! For those who have believed on and accepted Christ's free gift of salvation, we shall spend eternity with Him. The hope of spending eternity with the lover of my soul is enough to make my heart soar; however, the promise that not only will I spend it with Christ, but also with my children who have gone on ahead, makes me dance for joy. I will continue to boldly declare to anyone that my children are not only in my past, BUT they are in my future!

If you are unsure of your future, please consider praying the following prayer with a sincere heart:

Lord Jesus, I am unsure about my future.
I want to be sure. I am tired of trying to figure it all out. I
surrender my will to you.
Forgive me of trying to always do things my way.
I ask you to come into my life, be the Lord of my heart. I want to
do it your way. I receive your free gift of salvation. Thank you,
Jesus.

Welcome, friends, to the family! I am excited beyond measure to know that if we never meet on this planet, we will spend eternity getting to know each other. I encourage you to get a Bible and to start reading the incredible love letter written to you. God will reveal himself and His goodness to you.

He loves you immensely.

Blessings!

About the Author

Karrie is an author, speaker and ordained minister of the gospel. She and her husband have been married 21 years and have 3 living children. It is her desire to see others set free and walking in the fullness and freedom of Christ Jesus. To know and understand that He has given each of us a voice and that He intends us to use that voice to bring Him Glory. Through her trust in God she strives to encourage, educate and equip those around her.

If you wish to contact the author, you may send an email to the following email address:
vesselsofearth@gmail.com

Children of Healing

www.ingramcontent.com/pod-product-compliance
Lightning Source LLC
Chambersburg PA
CBHW061833040426
42447CB00012B/2945